To- Carl,

❖ STANDING TALL IN THE SHADOWS ❖

May all your trails be
happy ones!

God Bless,
Dick Baxter

STANDING TALL
IN THE SHADOWS

Memoirs of a Hollywood Manager

DICK BAXTER

BearManorMedia.com

Published by:

Bear Manor Media
PO Box 71426
Albany GA 31707

www.bearmanormedia.com
Book Design by Leila Joiner

Printed in the United States of America on acid-free paper

ISBN 978-1-59393-105-6
ISBN 1-59393-105-0

TABLE OF CONTENTS

ACKNOWLEDGEMENTS

GRATITUDE AND A HEARTFELT "THANK YOU" GO TO THE FOLLOWING people who helped me on this project: Brenda Baum, who helped so much with my photos; Craig A. Breit, M.A., Professor Theatre Communications, Cerritos Community College, Los Angeles.; Bonnie Churchill, columnist National News Syndicate/Communications International; Bill Erwin, actor and friend; Carolyn and William Hanneman, my sister and her husband, who helped with photos and family history; Rick Huff, producer/host.; Osie Jackson, co-author of the book, *Shaking Hands with Fame*; Andy Klotz, Publicity/Media Relations Director, Indiana State Fair Grounds; Jennie Knudsen, celebrity photographer; Sam Lovullo, producer *Hee Haw*, CBS-TV; Dan Quick, movie producer; A. Jody Williams, Copyright Coordinator, Detroit Free Press; LaRue & Nancy Horsley (Roy Rogers/Dale Evans Festival, Portsmouth, Ohio); and my wife, Ellie Baxter.

To my wife, Ellie, who taught me to believe,
who has always had me believing in love,
believing in friendships,
believing in hard work,
but most of all,
believing in our dear Lord.

INTRODUCTION

THE TITLE OF THIS BOOK CAME ABOUT BY MY CAREFULLY CONSIDERING my position as a personal manager of famous celebrities. I feel that I was extremely honored to represent these very popular world-famous personalities.

A personal manager should be the person in charge of any actor/entertainer's career. The artist is the corporation and the manager is like the CEO. On behalf of the artist and always in concert with the artist, he oversees the artist's career. He should have training in business and entertainment rules and laws. The manager and his client make all the decisions regarding the artist's press agents, recording contracts, bookings, business manager and booking agents. Client and artist should be a very close relationship, a business marriage of sorts.

A manager is there to manage their careers and protect them. It is never the manager, but the clients who shine brightly in their stardom. The manager, in his wisdom and know-how, must not stand in their glow of fame, but stand very tall and proud in their shadow.

CHAPTER 1

I WAS BORN IN A RURAL COMMUNITY, SHELBYVILLE, INDIANA, SOME 28 miles south east of Indianapolis, Indiana, in 1935. My parents, William and Alberta Baxter, already had three children, two girls, my sisters Jean and Carolyn, and brother, Harold. Seven years after my birth, my brother Wayne was born. We grew up in a farming community near Fairland, Indiana, one mile from where Marjorie Main, the famous actress (Ma Kettle of the *Ma & Pa Kettle* movies), had been born, at her father's farm, the Tomlinson Farm. I was a childhood chum of the grandson of one of Marjorie's childhood friends.

My parents were not farmers, however. My father was a furniture maker by trade and my mother a homemaker. This was long before women's lib, when women felt very comfortable and proud to stay home and take care of the home front. My paternal grandfather, William F. Baxter, was a contractor by trade and helped build many of the homes in and around Shelbyville. My maternal grandfather, Dr. Francis Dunn, was one of the early doctor/surgeons in Shelbyville and I guess my mother was secretly praying that I might be a doctor someday, but for me it just wasn't in the cards. I could not stand the sight of blood. Instead, at a very early age, I began to show a sincere interest in music and acting. Where did this desire come from? Well, my father's cousin was an actor and my mother's only sister was an actress/singer on Broadway. No one else in my family at that time or since has shown any interest in the entertainment business.

I'm not sure to this day that my family understands what I have been doing all these 37 years, but, I must say, they love me and they show sincere interest and care in mine and Ellie's life. We remain very close.

We have also been very close to Ellie's sister, Edna Jeanne, and until her mother's passing in 1998, Edna Landis was more than a mother-in-law to me. She was a second mom and very dear friend.

I grew up reading books like *The Bears of Blue River* by Charles Major (born in 1856) and listening to the Grand Ole Opry from Nashville, Tennessee. I listened intently to music by Hank Snow, Lulubelle & Scotty, Hank Williams, Eddy Arnold and all the country singers of that era. I also listened to pop and my favorites were Perry Como, Kate Smith, Jo Stafford, Doris Day and Buddy Clark. It was during this period, the early '40s, that with a pad and pencil in hand, I would go out far from the house and sit on a fence and create lyrics and poems. I must have been all of 12 years old. Yes, I even wrote love songs, but what does a boy of these young years understand about love? I wrote one song when I was about 14 years old titled "It's a Lovely Night for Lovers."

Some 18 years later a former producer at Capitol Records heard this song and wondered why I had not tried to get it recorded, but I was too embarrassed. These were the words of a 14-year-old, and I was now a successful manager. No, it would remain private to me and my family.

I was a BIG movie buff also and it was in 1943 that my mother took me to the Ritz Theater in Shelbyville to see a movie with her personal favorites Lulubelle & Scotty. The movie was Republic's *Swing Your Partner*, and also starring in this film was an actress/singer named Dale Evans.

I did not remember Lulubelle & Scotty that well after seeing the picture, but I certainly remembered this beautiful girl, Dale Evans, and I became a fan at eight years of age. I'm one of those people who was a fan long before her Western days as Roy Rogers' co-star and wife. (More about Dale later in this book, as I became a friend, and also her manager for about 14 years, throughout the '70s and early '80s.)

After high school, I moved to Indianapolis to take a business course at Manual Arts. It was during this period I got a job (my very first) at an insurance company as an underwriter. One of the employees there was this strikingly beautiful young girl who I took a liking to instantly. We would chat on breaks and back at the files where she worked. She was shy and I, a farm boy, was rather shy also. We just knew we liked each other. Now, in an office situation of about 30 employees, even back in the 1950s, people loved to gossip and play cupid. I was told by many employees that this girl, who I liked a lot, had a crush on me. In fact, she had made the remark on my first day at work, as I came off the elevator into the office area, that I was the man she was going to marry. What insight this lady had! She, after months of polite conversation, evidently got up enough nerve to invite me on an outing to Riverside Park (an amusement park with rides, etc.). Yes, she asked me out on our first date. I guess I was shy. I accepted eagerly. Am I glad I did, this girl is now my wife and best friend, Ellie. As of this writing we will celebrate 51 years of marriage on December 9, 2006. Ellie would also be the one to understand and help me with my decision to move to Southern California, only a short six years after our marriage. This was a huge sacrifice for us both. I would be leaving my family and would be leaving behind her beloved mother Edna and sister Edna Jeanne. In May 1961 to California we moved; lock, stock and barrel, for better or worse. We were determined to make a go of it.

Our first home was in Sherman Oaks, California. We rented a guest house from famed *Look* magazine photographer Earl Theisen and his wife Lillian.

We soon grew to love Earl and Lillian as our own family and spent many wonderful times together. After a couple of years, we got our home in Encino, California, a barn-red bat-n-board ranch house, on three-quarters of an acre. We really felt settled in now and this is the time when I started taking acting and voice lessons and planning a career in the entertainment business. As I will explain shortly, that faithful night at a nightclub in Encino seeing the Four Tunes was to change my career and life forever. Now, come join me on my journey into the world of entertainment.

CHAPTER 2

THE YEAR WAS 1963, AND MY WIFE ELLIE AND I HAD LIVED IN SOUTHERN California since May 1961, moving from Indiana, our birthplace. I was successful as a credit manager for an office furniture and supply company. Ellie was employed by a national insurance company. (Later, she was employed by NBC-TV in Burbank, California for 17 years. We were living in Encino, California at the time.)

One warm spring evening, friends of ours wanted us to join them at a nightclub located about one mile from our home. They said a fantastic R & B group was appearing for a short time in the lounge. We arrived just in time for the group's first set. To my surprise, the group turned out to be The Four Tunes, Liberty Records recording artists. Now, I had loved all forms of music since childhood and this was an act I could sit and listen to for hours. During one of their breaks, two of the members came over to speak to our friends. (I believe our friends had seen them perform before.) After being introduced to Jim Gordon, the leader of the group, Jim began to inquire about my interest in music and what I was currently doing for a living. When I explained that I was in credit management and had a solid background in business management, Jim said, "Dick, you would be a great personal manager for us." Personal management of talent? What was that? Jim asked for my business card, we watched another set and we bid goodnight and left.

A few days later at my home, I received a call from Jim. Had I given any thought to managing the group? I had not, but now I was getting curious.

It just happened that former neighbors of ours in Sherman Oaks, California, Art and Edna Whiting, were longtime booking agents with great success. I called Edna and asked if I might come over and speak to them in regards to this "personal management" thing. Edna and Art were happy to see me and were able to explain valuable information regarding personal management of talent and show business in general. They were pros!

It was decided that if I chose to give it a try, the Whitings would sponsor me, getting my license with our local Musicians Union. In those days the Musicians Union licensed personal managers. So it came to be that I established Dick Baxter Management in 1963, The Four Tunes being my first clients. I placed them with the Whitings for bookings. From this period on, I took on new clients, both singers and actors. I seemed to be on my way. I was constantly filled with doubts as to how my career had taken such a drastic change. I was successful, but deep down inside I wondered if I should not be doing something more worthwhile with my life. Ellie was very supportive and gave me faith and courage to believe in what I was now pursuing.

It is now the early 1970s, the place, an auditorium in Orange County, California. The auditorium was fast filling up with anxious spectators here to see one of America's legends in Country/Gospel music, Stuart Hamblen. Stuart, the composer of such greats as "This Ole House," "It is No Secret What God Can Do," "Remember Me, I'm the One Who Loves You," and the list goes on. In the control booth the engineers were working on our sound check, backstage people were busying themselves with activity in preparation for Stuart's concert to begin.

The person in charge, making sure that the concert would be perfect, or as near-perfect as possible for the fans, was Stuart's personal manager, Dick Baxter. Stuart and I had gotten together as client/manager only a year or so before this night.

Also being represented by me was Stuart's partner and loving wife, Suzy. Suzy, a songwriter and performer herself, would be on the program tonight.

Now having been a personal manager of entertainers since 1964 and doing very well, I got to thinking about my life. Maybe it was the spiritual quality of this arena or I was just feeling tired. At that time in my career I was working seven days a week and sometimes 12 to 14 hours a day. I began to think, Dick Baxter, you are just a young man from the farmlands of Indiana. Your father was a cabinet maker by trade, your mother a devoted wife, mother and homemaker. Your father's father was a contractor and built many homes in the small rural town of Shelbyville, Indiana where you were born. Your maternal grandfather, Dr. Francis Dunn, was one of the early MDs and surgeons in Shelbyville. How your mother would have loved to see you follow in the footsteps of her father and be a doctor. You have two sisters and two brothers and none of them had the "crazy" notion of "showbiz." But, wait, a cousin of your father's was an actor and your mother's only sister had been an actress and singer on Broadway. You see, I did have it in my blood. These thoughts were swiftly going through my mind as I watched this fevered activity going on backstage at this auditorium some 2,000 miles from where my life began. I had doubts. What am I doing in show business? I expressed this quietly to Suzy. Suzy said gently, "Dick, look out here," as she carefully pulled a small portion of the stage curtain back. "See all those faces." By this time the auditorium was packed (and I later was advised that some were turned away). Suzy continued, "Through your efforts, you have brought Stuart Hamblen's show here tonight. You see, some of these people have come just to be entertained for 1½ hours and forget their hurts, disappointments and worries. Hopefully their hearts will be lighter when they leave this auditorium and though they have come to see Stuart, you are a big part of this happiness. That is why you are here; this, for now, is where God wants you."

That night was the beginning of no more doubts for me. I thought, I chose to be a personal manager of talent years ago and God gave me all these opportunities and talent to be the best I can be. For this is my calling and, throughout the years, I have been very fortunate to work with wonderful talent and great caring, God-fearing people like Stuart, Anacani (a singer from the Lawrence Welk TV Show), Hi Busse & The Frontiersmen & Joanie, Dale Evans, Roy Rogers, Jr., and The Four Tunes.

CHAPTER 3

Brief Encounter with A Hollywood Icon

EARLY IN MY CAREER, I HAD GONE TO THE LARGE BANK BUILDING AT Hollywood & Vine for an appointment regarding one of my clients. I stepped onto one of the elevators and pushed the button for my desired floor. The only other person on the elevator with me was a smartly dressed lady wearing a huge hat. She smiled as I got on the elevator and, as the doors closed, we began to ascend to the upper floors. All of a sudden the elevator stopped, and she spoke to me for the first time. She let out a retort of "What the hell happened?" That's when I recognized this lady as one of Hollywood's most famous and colorful columnists, Hedda Hopper. I replied with "I'm not sure," and at that moment the elevator began to move once again.

I had met up with the famous Hedda Hopper. She and another columnist, Louella Parsons (1881-1972), ruled the gossip and news in Hollywood in the golden era. Hedda (1885-1966) was known for her large flamboyant hats and that day she certainly was wearing one of her famous trademarks.

A very brief encounter, but I enjoyed meeting one of Hollywood's most famous ladies.

CHAPTER 4

I Didn't Want To Do a TV Talk Show, Anyway

A SHORT TIME AFTER I FOUNDED MY PERSONAL MANAGEMENT COMPANY, Dick Baxter Management, a TV producer had heard about me and thought I would be good as a TV talk show host, in the style of Merv Griffin and Mike Douglas. He and some writer convinced me to do the pilot. I never gave up my management company, as I was not sure I would like being in front of the cameras. A script was written and guest comic Marty Allen and songstress Joanie Summers were signed to be my guests on the pilot. They decided the TV pilot would be shot at Bell Movie Ranch near Chatsworth, California.

Tom Giganti was hired as my make-up man, the director was set and we were ready for the filming. On the morning of the shoot, I had forgotten the wardrobe I was to wear, brown western dress slacks and a beige corduroy sport coat. This held up the start time while someone went to my home to gather my wardrobe. Finally, we were ready for the shoot. Bell Movie Ranch has been the location for such TV shows as *The Big Valley*, with Barbara Stanwyck, and many others. It was a very fun place to be as it was an old Western town setting.

My talk show was to have a country/western feel. Marty Allen and I did a comedy sketch about Marty robbing the local bank. It turned out okay and Marty was a real pro working with me, a beginner. I interviewed Joanie Summers and she sang a couple of songs.

The day had gone reasonably smooth and the pilot was finished. Now it was up to the producer to try and sell the pilot, intended for syndication. He flew to New York, showed the pilot around. One sponsor liked what they saw, but they felt I came across as too inexperienced, but would be interested in seeing more of my work on film. This was not where I wished to be. I declined and never looked back, as I enjoyed working behind the scenes and especially working with wonderful talented artists. Management was not the only career I had chosen, but I enjoyed the challenges.

CERRITOS COMMUNITY COLLEGE DISTRICT
11110 ALONDRA BLVD. • NORWALK, CALIFORNIA 90650-6298 • (310) 860-2451• FAX (310) 467-5005

5 November 1996

To Whom It May Concern:

I have had the distinct pleasure of knowing and working with Mr. Dick Baxter in both a personal and professional setting since 1980. Dick brings a unique combination of professional managerial experience and warm wise counsel each time he visits my students.

Since the aforementioned date, I have taught courses in Mass Communication, Radio Production, Introduction to Broadcasting, Public Speaking and Interpersonal Communication at Cerritos, Orange Coast, Long Beach State and Santa Ana Colleges. Dick Baxter has literally talked to dozens of my students in the management unit, each time leaving them wanting more.

As a guest speaker, Mr. Baxter exhibits the enthusiasm, competence and approachability that works well on the lecture circuit. Blending facts, figures, technique along with tons of personal anecdotes, he captures attention from the first to the last breath. Moreover, Dick helps create real interest in the entertainment industry. I can tell from watching students and their reactions to him. They frequently won't let him go. Dick Baxter is a hard act to follow.

Dick Baxter has worked with a list of luminaries in the entertainment business second to none. Dick Baxter is also a star in his own right. Try him and see.

I intend to watch Dick Baxter's future with great interest. You would do well to make him a part of yours.

Sincerely,

Craig A. Breit, M.A.
Professor, Theatre-Communications

Dick Baxter Publishing Company

(Ascap)

Most Notable Songs And Compositions

Promises To Keep

The Miracle Of Miracles

MY BELOVED MOTHER, ALBERTA DUNN BAXTER
1908 – 1969

My handsome Father,
William Baxter, Age 21 years
1892 – 1962

ELLIE'S MOTHER, EDNA LANDIS
1903 – 1998

MY SISTER CAROLYN HANNEMAN, HER HUSBAND BILL,
AND SONS RANDAL AND MICHAEL WAYNE

MY BROTHER, WAYNE BAXTER

MY FATHER'S FRIEND, PETE TREON, MY DAD, AND YOURS TRULY. THISE RABBITS WERE ALMOST BIGGER THAN I WAS.

A HIGH SCHOOL PHOTO. I'M 16 YEARS OLD.

DICK, AGE 18

HERE I AM WITH MY BABY
BROTHER, WAYNE.
HE'S 7 YEARS YOUNGER.

OUR WEDDING PORTRAIT, DECEMBER 9, 1955

OUR FIRST ANNIVERSARY, DECEMBER 9, 1956

Our Twelfth Year Together as
Mr. and Mrs. Baxter

ELLIE AND I HAVE BEEN MARRIED TWELVE YEARS.
THE YEAR, 1967.

OUR SILVER WEDDING ANNIVERSARY
1980

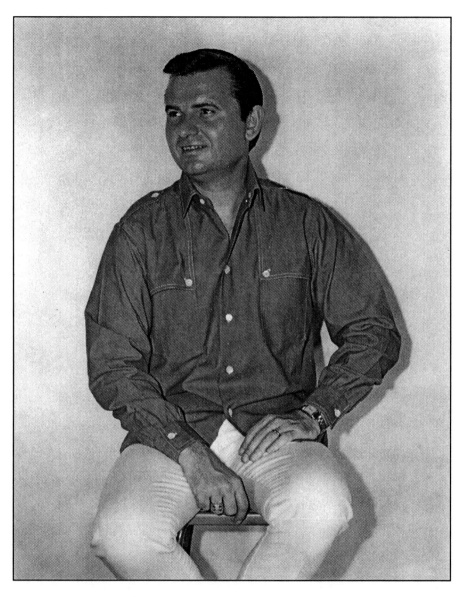

A VERY EARLY PUBLICITY PHOTO.
1962

ANOTHER PUBLICITY SHOT – 1962.

YET ANOTHER PUBLICITY
PHOTO – 1962.

SEE HOW SERIOUS I CAN BE.

DICK AS A MODEL FOR
VIOLA GRAE WESTERN
WEAR.

AD AND PHOTO APPEARED
IN *WESTERN HORSEMAN*
MAGAZINE, MAY 1965.

ROY ROGERS, ELLIE BAXTER, DICK AND DALE EVANS
AT THE INDIANA STATE FAIR, 1956.

AN OUTING AT KNOTT'S BERRY FARM IN CALIFORNIA.
DODIE ROGERS (ROY AND DALE'S DAUGHTER), ELLIE, DICK, AND
YES, THE MONSTER HIMSELF, FRANKENSTEIN. EARLY 1960'S.

AVERY NEAT PHOTO. DICK IN THE MID-1960'S, PHOTOGRAPHED ACROSS FROM THE ORIGINAL ROY ROGERS AND DALE EVANS MUSEUM IN APPLE VALLEY, CALIFORNIA.

PHOTO TAKEN IN 1961 IN
SHERMAN OAKS BY FAMOUS
LOOK MAGAZINE
PHOTOGRAPHER, EARL
THEISEN.

ONE OF MY PERSONAL FAVORITE PHOTOS
OF ELLIE AND I.
BRENTWOOD, CALIFORNIA – 1970'S.

PASADENA, CALIFORNIA IN THE 1970'S.
MY FAVORITE PHOTO OF MY LADY AND I.

PHOTO TAKEN BY MY DEAR FRIEND, HOLLYWOOD PHOTOGRAPHER
BOB BUCHER. BOB HAD BEEN WITH CBS-RADIO FOR YEARS.

PHOTO THAT APPEARS IN THE KINGSBURY EDITION OF
WHO'S WHO IN COUNTRY AND WESTERN MUSIC, 1981.

MY LONGTIME DEAR FRIEND, BONNIE CHURCHILL, AND MYSELF,
BONNIE'S SISTER, REBA, ROY ROGERS AND A FRIEND OF THE
CHURCHILL'S. PHOTO TAKEN IN ROY AND DALE'S HOME IN
APPLE VALLEY, CALIFORNIA – 1980'S.

ELLIE'S SISTER, EDNA J., ELLIE, DICK AND ELLIE'S MOTHER
AT OUR HOME IN SHERMAN OAKS, CALIFORNIA – 1978.

ELLIE'S FAVORITE PHOTO OF HER HUSBAND! 1990'S.

ELLIE AND DICK
VACATIONING IN PALM
SPRINGS, CALIFORNIA IN THE
1960'S.

EARLY PHOTO OF COUNTRY/GOSPEL GREAT,
STUART HAMBLEN, AND HIS BAND.

A VERY GOOD-LOOKING COUPLE, MY FRIENDS AND CLIENTS,
SUZY AND STUART HAMBLEN.

THIS PHOTO HUNG IN MY OFFICE AT DICK BAXTER MANAGEMENT.
ONE OF MY PERSONAL FAVORITES.

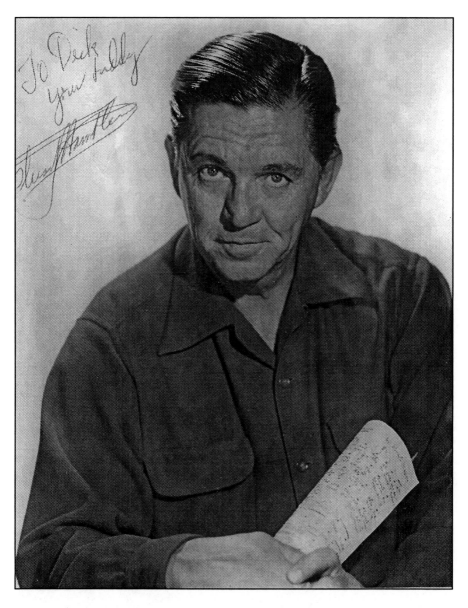

THIS AUTOGRAPH SAYS IT ALL. WE WERE GOOD FRIENDS.
I MISS STUART VERY MUCH.

A GREAT LADY AND MY FRIEND, SUZY HAMBLEN.

Concert at the Civic Auditorium, Pasadena, California.
Stuart Hamblen, Dick, and Suzy Hamblen.

STUART AND ACTRESS JANE WITHERS ON KLAC RADIO IN
LOS ANGELES. THE MAN STANDING BEHIND STUART IS
PUBLICIST SAM BENSON, A GOOD FRIEND.

STUART'S RADIO SHOW, "COWBOY CHURCH OF THE AIR,"
WAS SYNDICATED AND AIRED IN LOS ANGELES ON KLAC-RADIO.

"I WON'T WEAR OVERALLS."
BUT HE DID AND HAD A BLAST!
STUART WITH COUNTRY GREAT, BUCK OWENS,
ON CBS-TV's *HEE HAW* SHOW – 1970's.

THE LAST PUBLICITY PHOTO I HAD BOB BUCHER TAKE OF THE
HAMBLENS. PHOTO TAKEN IN NORTH HOLLYWOOD, CALIFORNIA IN
THE VERY EARLY 1980's.

DICK WITH FRIEND AND CLIENT,
COUNTRY/GOSPEL SINGER JUNE WADE

DICK WITH FRIEND AND CLIENT, DALE EVANS.
PHOTO TAKEN IN SAN FERNANDO VALLEY IN 1977.
A 16X20 OF THIS PHOTO HAS HUNG IN MY OFFICE
EVER SINCE IT WAS TAKEN.

DICK, DALE EVANS, AND ELLIE AT A VERY EARLY
DOVE AWARDS SHOW IN SOUTHERN CALIFORNIA.

DALE EVANS

Personal Management
DICK BAXTER
(213) 782-9739
787-6509

THERE HAVE BEEN MANY, BUT THIS IS
ONE OF MY FAVORITE PHOTOS OF DALE.

DALE EVANS

Personal Management
DICK BAXTER
(213) 782-9739
787-6509

PUBLICITY PHOTO OF DALE – 1976.

A VERY GLAMOROUS DALE.
PHOTO TAKEN FOR DICK BAXTER MANAGEMENT IN 1977.

DALE EVANS

NOONTIME SHOW ON CBS-TV IN LOS ANGELES.

BACKSTAGE AT THE DINAH SHORE TV SHOW.
ART RUSH (ROY ROGER'S MANAGER), DALE EVANS, ROY ROGERS,
AND DICK BAXTER (DALE'S MANAGER).

I HAD THIS PICTURE OF DALE TAKEN IN 1977.

FRAN ERWIN (TV EDITOR, *DAILY NEWS*), DICK,
AND DALE EVANS TAKEN AFTER AN INTERVIEW
AT THE TAIL OF THE COCK RESTAURANT,
STUDIO CITY, CALIFORNIA

DUSTY ROGERS, DICK, DALE EVANS, ROY ROGERS, AND
RECORD PRODUCER TRACY DART AT CONTRACT SIGNING
FOR ALBUM, "HAPPY TRAILS."

BACKSTAGE IN LAS VEGAS. ELLIE, DALE, AND LINDA
(DUSTY ROGER'S WIFE). DUSTY WAS APPEARING AT
SAM'S TOWN HOTEL CASINO

THE WHOLE GANG – DUSTY, LINDA, ROY, DALE, ELLIE, AND DICK
AT SAM'S TOWN IN LAS VEGAS.

DALE IN LONE PINE, CALIFORNIA.
PHOTO TAKEN BY MY DEAR FRIEND,
CELEBRITY PHOTOGRAPHER JENNIE KNUDSEN.

ROY ROGERS JR.

Personal Management
DICK BAXTER
(213) 782-9739
787-6509

PHOTO SHOT BY BOB BUCHER
FOR PUBLICITY FOR DICK BAXTER MANAGEMENT.

MY LONGTIME FRIEND, PHOTOGRAPHER BOB BUCHER, DUSTY ROGERS, AND ME AT A PHOTO SHOOT IN NORTH HOLLYWOOD, CALIFORNIA

TAKEN AT DUSTY'S RECORDING SESSION FOR HIS ALBUM, "JUST CALL ME DUSTY," IN HOLLYWOOD, CALIFORNIA. SAGE AND SOUND STUDIOS.

ANACANI GAVE ELLIE AND ME THIS AUTOGRAPHED PHOTO AT
THE BEGINNING OF OUR CLIENT/MANAGER RELATIONSHIP.

STORE MANAGERS, DICK, ANACANI, SALES REP, AND JAIMIE,
ANACANI'S RECORD PRODUCER AT A RECORD SIGNING,
DOWNTOWN LOS ANGELES.

DICK AND CLIENT ANACANI,
SHERMAN OAKS, CALIFORNIA - 1981

DICK, ANACANI, AND RECORD PRODUCER,
JAIMIE.

ANACANI

ANACANI GROWS MORE BEAUTIFUL WITH EACH PASSING YEAR.
SHE SENT ME THIS PHOTO TO USE IN THIS BOOK.
YES, WE STILL KEEP IN TOUCH.
ELLIE AND I LOVE HER AND HER FAMILY.

DICK BAXTER — JOANIE HALL — HI BUSSE

"THE FRONTIERSMEN" and joanie

Personal Management
DICK BAXTER
(213) 782-9739
787-6509

PUBLICITY PHOTO TAKEN FOR DICK BAXTER MANAGEMENT,
LATE 1970'S.

HI BUSSE

Personal Management
DICK BAXTER
(213) 782-9739
787-6509

HE WAS AFFECTIONATELY CALLED HI POCKETS.
HE WAS ONE OF THE MOST GENTLE GENTLEMEN I EVER MET.
AND I WAS PROUD TO BE HIS MANAGER FOR A TIME.

Joanie Hall

Personal Management
DICK BAXTER
(213) 782-9739
787-6509

ELLIE AND I REMAIN FRIENDS WITH JOANIE, AND WE TALK BY
PHONE OFTEN. SHE LIVES ABOUT 150 MILES AWAY FROM US,
SO WE DO NOT SEE HER AS MUCH AS WE WOULD LIKE.

WAYNE WEST — JOANIE HALL — HI BUSSE
THE FRONTIERSMEN AND JOANIE

AT OUR 25TH WEDDING ANNIVERSARY.
ELLIE AND JOANIE,
SHERMAN OAKS, CALIFORNIA

Peggy Coburn

PEGGY KEEPS IN TOUCH. WE SPEAK AT LEAST EVERY TWO WEEKS.
ONE OF OUR MOST CHERISHED AND DEAR FRIENDS
FOR OVER 30 YEARS.

Gloria Jean

Personal Management
DICK BAXTER
(213) 782-9739
787-6509

GLORIA WAS A FAMOUS CHILD STAR. SHE HAS REMAINED CLOSE TO
ELLIE AND I FOR OVER 35 YEARS. WE LOVE HER AND HER SISTER,
BONNIE, AND VALUE THEIR FRIENDSHIP.

Catherine McLeod

Personal Management
DICK BAXTER
(213) 782-9739
787-6509

CATHERINE LIVED NEAR ELLIE AND I WHEN WE LIVED IN SHERMAN OAKS, CALIFORNIA.

Two of my favorite people, Fran and Bill Erwin.
Fran is no longer with us. I miss her.
Bill is a longtime actor, whom I am sure you recognize.

"Tough Men," starring Bill Erwin and Ken Edwards

ONE OF HOLLYWOOD'S TRUE GREATS.
A KIND, LOVING LADY AND OUR GOOD FRIEND.

KATHRYN GRAYSON

ROY ROGERS LOOK-ALIKE, BILL NOLT.
BILL AND HIS WIFE, DONENE, ARE GOOD FRIENDS.
[PHOTO: JENNIE KNUDSEN]

ACTRESS DONNA MARTELL
MADE HER FILM DEBUT IN
ROY AND DALE'S MOVIE,
"APACHE ROSE."
[PHOTO: JENNIE KNUDSEN]

CHAPTER 5

Stuart Hamblen

A man of great talent, strength, integrity, and kindness.

One of America's greatest Country/Gospel recording artists, and beloved songwriters.

He and his wife, Suzy, two of my dearest and most cherished friends.

Actor, singer, songwriter and my friend. Let me tell you about my friend and client, Stuart Hamblen.

Stuart was born Carl Stuart Hamblen in Kellyville, Texas, on October 20, 1908, the son of an itinerant Methodist preacher, J.H. Hamblen. He went to McMurray State Teachers College in Abilene, Texas. For a short time after graduation, Stuart did in fact teach school. Along the way, this tall, ruggedly handsome man, who stood 6'2", also was a cow puncher, a race horse trainer and became one of America's favorite composers/singers and one of our greatest country/gospel recording artists.

Stuart was a man of great strength, integrity and kindness. I learned that he was very honest and you could trust his very word. The 14 years we were together was just on a handshake. No contract was involved, just two guys who believed in each others' abilities.

Stuart was barely 20 years old when he signed his first recording contract with RCA-Victor. Finding no real interest in teaching or other jobs, Stuart, with his Victor contract, knew that his professional career had to be in music.

At a very young age, Stuart moved to Hollywood, California as a member of a touring/singing group known as The Beverly Hillbillies. He soon began a successful radio program, *Stuart Hamblen and his Lucky Stars*, as a result of his singing career. The program was very popular on the west coast and set national records for longevity. Stuart was featured on the program singing, joking around with his guests and other members of his show. A member of his band was a very young Cliffie Stone. (More on Cliffie later.)

In April 1933, Stuart married the petite and very pretty Suzy Daniels. (Suzy was also a client of mine. Suzy wrote songs and did speaking engagements on Inspirational Living.) The couple had two daughters, Veeva and Lisa, and it is Lisa who introduced me to her father in the late 1960s.

Lisa and I were working together and one day Lisa mentioned that she would like me to meet her father. She said he was a famous singer & songwriter and maybe he would be interested in my managing his career. That evening I was speaking on the phone with my mother, back in Indiana, and I mentioned that I might meet with Stuart Hamblen. She was thrilled, as Stuart happened to be one of my folks' favorite recording artists. She seemed to know something about this Stuart

Hamblen person. My folks liked the artist; maybe I would like the man. Lisa set up the meeting.

That evening, Ellie and I headed up to their home in the Hollywood Hills, in the San Fernando Valley, about a half-hour drive from our home. (This house had a history; we later learned it had been previously owned by the famous actor Errol Flynn. It was very well known in the Hollywood community.) Upon arriving at this very huge, beautiful estate, we were immediately met by the Hamblens' very friendly black labs. Met at the door by Suzy & Stuart, we immediately felt at home. The Hamblens were warm, gracious hosts. We were guided to the huge studio where Stuart worked on his music and various projects on a daily basis. We were given coffee by the Hamblens' maid and we were ready to learn about this fascinating man. He spoke to me as though we were old friends. We instantly clicked. I learned that evening that Stuart was the composer of the huge hit "This Ole House" on RCA-Victor. I had seen it performed on the *Your Hit Parade* TV show many times. "This Ole House" was awarded song of the year in 1958. It was recorded by Stuart, Rosemary Clooney and other artists of that time.

I had met songstress Gisele MacKenzie, star of the *Hit Parade* TV show, sometime back. One day I saw her at one of our local stores. She called to me, "Dick, did I ever tell you how many times I had to perform 'This Ole House' on the *Hit Parade* show?" It remained in the top songs for something like 40 weeks. Thus, the popularity of this hit song. I learned about many of Stuart's songs, which I realized I had heard before. Songs like, "His Hands," "Until Then," "Open Up Your Heart (And Let the Sunshine In)," "How Big is God," "I've Got So Many Million Years," and "It Is No Secret (What God Can Do)."

I was also to learn this evening how the song "It Is No Secret" came to be written. One evening Stuart & Suzy were guests at a party at the home of actor John Wayne. Wayne noticed that Stuart had lost his taste for alcohol. Upon parting, the actor asked Stuart how he broke himself from alcohol. "I didn't do it," Stuart replied, "The Lord did it. It's no secret what God can do in our lives." Stuart recalled that when he and Suzy arrived home, the chimes of their Grandfather Clock in the hall struck midnight and in seventeen minutes he had composed the lyrics and tune. It has been one of Stuart's best selling and loved songs. This story of "It Is No Secret" is told in author Dorothy

Horstman's book *Sing Your Heart Out, Country Boy* (E.P. Dutton & Co., Inc., New York, 1975).

I was also made aware of Stuart's movie work. Stuart was under contract to Republic Pictures (yes, the same studio where Roy Rogers and later Dale Evans was). From 1937 to 1950 Stuart did over nine films at the studio including, In Old Monterey with Gene Autry, *The Arizona Kid* and *King of the Cowboys* with Roy Rogers, *The Sombrero Kid* with Don "Red" Barry, *Plainsman and the Lady* with Bill Elliott and Vera Ralston (the wife of Republic's head, Herbert Yates. I was to meet both Vera and Herbert in later years), and a serial, *King of the Forest Rangers*. Most of these films are either on VHS or DVD. You will find more material on Stuart's film career in Jack Mathis' books, *Republic Confidential - The Players* (1992) and *Republic Confidential - The Studio* (1999).

Suzy served us all the best Peach cobbler I'd had since my childhood in Indiana. Before we left that night, Stuart and I shook hands and agreed to be manager and client. This lasted for over 14 years.

Shortly after I became Stuart's manager, a local country/western radio station in Los Angeles asked Stuart to do a radio program. The new program would be called *Cowboy Church on the Air* and would broadcast every Sunday morning. Stuart starred and played music by various artists like Mahalia Jackson, Pat Boone, Roy Rogers & Dale Evans and his own recordings. The show became very popular in and around the Los Angeles area.

Soon, we were approached to syndicate the series and the show was soon heard not only in California, but Oregon, Washington, Arizona and many Western states. We received much mail from listeners and were thrilled it was being accepted very favorably. We had the shows duplicated at a recording studio in Glendale, California, about 10 miles from Stuart's home.

One morning I stopped at the studio in Glendale to pick up the reels of duplication. Not realizing how heavy they were, I assured the man that handled the radio transcripts that I could carry them to my car. Oh boy, were they heavy! Later that day I began to experience pain and hurting in my left shoulder. I was sure the pain would pass, as I figured I had just strained my arms by carrying the tapes. No, the pain did not ease up, so I decided I must see my doctor. An examination at the doctor's office indicated I had bursitis.

Seeing Stuart for a business meeting the next morning, he wanted to know what my doctor found out. I told him bursitis. And what kind of mediation did he prescribe? Stuart wanted to know. I explained I was given a prescription of Butezolidin. "Hey, man," Stuart exclaimed, "that's what they give my race horses." We both had a laugh over this.

Stuart owned race horses and one of the most famous was El Lobo. A beautiful picture of El Lobo was displayed proudly in the Hamblens' den.

Some weekends, Stuart, Suzy, Ellie and I would drive down to see the horses and their trainer. We'd then stop someplace on the way back to Hollywood and have a nice lunch and Stuart would relate stories of his past adventures. He was a marvelous storyteller, as good as Will Rogers, I believe. Ellie and I still cherish those moments of closeness to Stuart & Suzy.

The show boosted renewed interest in Stuart and it wasn't very long until I was getting requests for his appearance at churches, concert halls, festivals, etc. One of the personal appearances we did was the concert I mentioned earlier in this book. Many shows followed. I recall one concert in particular. I had arranged for Stuart to appear at the convention center of a large hotel in Ventura, California. Ellie and I were going up to the concert via one of the elevators in the hotel. Riding the elevator with us was country great Johnny Cash. Johnny and Stuart knew each other very well and when Johnny heard from me that Stuart was appearing here at the convention center, he joined us and later went up on the stage with Stuart and they did a song together. You can't buy memories like this.

Another engagement that stands out in my mind was the Pasadena, California Civic Auditorium show in the mid-'70s. Stuart shared this program with another, Corrie Ten Boom. She had written "The Hiding Place," which later became a movie. Miss Ten Boom was a Dutch lady that survived the Holocaust.

Today, her museum stands in Haarlem, Holland. She was in her 80s and the most gracious, energetic woman I had ever met. Now, I had met actors, singers, religious leaders and sports figures, but I was absolutely spellbound by Ms. Ten Boom. Miss Ten Boom was born in Holland, April 15, 1892, and passed away on April 18, 1983. What a legacy she has left!

The concerts and the radio show created interest in Stuart to record a new album. I set a deal with a producer for Stuart to record some of his best-known songs, "This Ole House," "My Mary," etc. The producer, Martin Haerle, wanted to record in Nashville. Now, this could present a problem, as Stuart had always recorded at Columbia & RCA in Hollywood. How would I sell Stuart on the idea of Nashville? I hit it head-on with the idea it would be good for his career, as we would get a lot of publicity as it was his first time to record in Nashville and he would be on the Grand Ole Opry while we were there. Stuart was somewhat reluctant, but he and Suzy trusted my judgment, so it was a done deal.

To Nashville we would go. The year was 1974 and fall was coming on, so we would finish and be back home for the holiday season. When we got to Nashville, we would be recording at Billy Linneman's Hilltop Studios. The morning we left L.A. International Airport, we were waiting for our flight in the VIP waiting room. Minnie Pearl (of Grand Ole Opry fame), Governor Dunn of Tennessee and security men were also waiting for the same flight. Minnie had been out in L.A. to attend actor Jim Nabors' party the night before. Soon our flight was called and we would be on our way to Nashville, Stuart, Suzy and I.

Upon arrival in Nashville, we bid goodbye to Minnie, Governor Dunn and the secret service men. We were then transported to our hotel where we would be housed for the next 10 days. After we were settled in our rooms, Stuart and Suzy in their room and me across the hall, we decided it was time for dinner. Stuart wanted to stay in their room and watch a football game on TV. So it was decided that Suzy and I would go out to dinner and bring Stuart's food back to him.

The clerk at the hotel gave Suzy and me a name of a restaurant he felt we might like. We ordered a cab (as we had not gotten a rental car) and were driven to this restaurant which had been recommended. When we arrived at the restaurant, we realized the cafй was a truck stop, but, I must admit, an upscale truck stop. Well, we are here, why not go in and have a bite to eat and get back to the hotel. The restaurant was very busy with truckers, tourists and locals. We took our seats and ordered our meals. Suzy wore a beautiful fur coat (after all, this was November in Tennessee and a good chill in the evening air) and I was in a business suit. Here's this older attractive lady with a much younger man, what a sight we must have made.

After finishing our meals and gathering up the food we would take back to Stuart, I paid our bill and proceeded to leave. While waiting for a cab to get us back to the hotel, we noticed to the right of us was a very nice gift shop. We visited the shop and, while looking around, I found a wonderful leather belt with a great silver buckle. I thought about buying it, but I looked at Suzy and said, "Oh, I think I will wait. We probably will come back here before we leave Nashville." Suzy looked up at me and in a very serious tone said, "Dick, I don't see why we would." We both had a laugh over that and soon our cab arrived.

On our return to the hotel we got a big shock, as the hotel doors were all locked (except one that was heavily guarded). What had happened? We were advised that there had been a murder and burglary in Nashville of one of Nashville's favorite performers. Some person or persons had killed Stringbean, a banjo player on the *Hee Haw* TV series (1969-1974), and his wife. The hotel was heavily guarded as several country/western artists were staying there, Tex Ritter, Johnny Bond and, of course, Stuart. The hotel, through their efforts, provided safety for all.

The next morning, Stuart wanted me to rent a car for our transportation from the hotel and trip around Nashville. Well, I've always been thrifty, so I selected a medium-size auto. This proved to be a bad choice as Stuart stood about 6'2" in stocking feet and built like John Wayne.

The very first day I drove us to Hilltop Recording Studio. As I parked in the artist parking lot, a Cadillac driven by Johnny Bond and his passenger, Tex Ritter (who were recording in one of the studios this day), parked right along side of our car. As Stuart descended from the passenger side of our vehicle (and it was an effort on Stuart's part), he exclaimed to Tex and Johnny, "Look what Dick did to me!" We all had a hearty laugh and proceeded into the studio.

Now it was time to go to work, Stuart and the musicians, the producer, engineer and myself in the control booth. The first day went very well. The musicians in Nashville are tremendously talented. The next day I had a visitor who had come to hear Stuart and visit with me in the control booth, Del Wood.

Del was a recording artist and pianist on the Grand Ole Opry show. It was fun and nice to have Del join us. Del was a very talented lady, pure country, funny and she became a good friend.

Also, during our stay in Nashville, I had the pleasure of visiting with Jo Walker, Executive Director of the Country Music Association. I also had the extreme pleasure of seeing the Ryman Auditorium (original home of the Grand Ole Opry), where so many country greats had appeared. Also, there was a brief visit to the famous Tootsie's Orchard Lounge nightspot.

I had arranged a press conference to announce that Stuart was recording in Nashville. The morning of the press interview, we had a writer from the *Nashville Banner*, syndicated writers and radio and TV. Stuart was center stage, so to speak, while Suzy and I sat off to one side allowing the press people to have access to him. Stuart started the interview with, "I'm not much for interviews, so I want you all to know this is Dick's idea." Suzy looked at me and whispered, "Couldn't you just kill him?" The fact was, we both knew Stuart well and, therefore, later we just had a good laugh. The press conference paid off; we got great newspaper, radio and TV coverage. After all, it was BIG news that country/gospel great Stuart Hamblen was recording in Nashville for the first time ever.

Saturday night, Stuart appeared on the Grand Ole Opry TV show and was very well received.

Time to pack up and leave Nashville as Stuart's album was finished after about 10 days. We had a good album; it was released under the title *The Man & His Music*. We would all be back home with our families for Thanksgiving.

After the holiday, I had an appointment at KLAC Radio, regarding Stuart's program, *The Cowboy Church*. While waiting in the outer waiting room to speak with Sam Benson, publicist for KLAC, country/western artist Lacy J. Dalton ("Crazy Blue Eyes," etc.) came in for an appointment. Sam introduced us, she was charming. It was a pleasure to meet her. Lacy was named Best New Female Vocalist in 1979 by the Academy of Country Music.

The '70s were busy years for Stuart and me. Stuart was honored on February 13, 1976 by the Los Angeles City Council when they named that day "Stuart Hamblen Day." This same year, Stuart was awarded a star on the famous Hollywood Walk of Fame.

Also in the '70s, CBS-TV had a very successful television show *Hee Haw*. It starred Buck Owens and Roy Clark. Also on the weekly show were Minnie Pearl, Lulu Roman, Grandpa Jones and other well-known country artists. Each week they also had special guest stars. It was their practice to dress the stars in bibbed overalls and place them in a corn-field setting to do jokes and gags. I thought *Hee Haw* was the perfect show for Stuart to be seen on. It had big ratings and was very popular with country/western audiences. Stuart was booked on the show, but he advised me that if I wanted him to do this show, he in no way was dressing in the overalls and doing this bit. Stuart was a man of great pride and dignity. I advised him that all guest stars did this, stars like George Jones, Roy Rogers & Dale Evans, and had great fun doing so.

Came the day to tape the show, and, of course, they wanted Stuart for one of the bits to be in those overalls. Reluctantly, Stuart, being a professional, obliged. He did the bit, overalls and all, and he had a ball. I was terribly relieved that all went well.

In the very early '80s, 1982 I recall, I had another client booked in the main showroom of a large hotel/casino in northern Nevada. In the past I had other clients appear at this hotel, so the owner/booker knew me pretty well and knew Stuart had been with me a long time.

They seemed to have a lot of visitors who liked Stuart's music and would love to see him in person. One day I got a call in my room that one of the owners wanted me to stop in their office. The meeting was regarding Stuart. Would I be interested in Stuart and his group of mu-sicians doing a few days in the main showroom? How could I ap-proach Stuart or even consider Stuart appearing at a hotel/casino? I declined, but on my return to my office in Los Angeles, I received calls wanting me to reconsider. Finally, I said we might come for a Friday and Saturday night show only. They had wanted a week. Also, I set the price very high, so they might back down. But, to my surprise, they accepted my deal and wanted to set a date for his appearance. How could I go to Stuart and explain I had this fantastic offer?

It turned out extremely well for Stuart, Suzy and their band. We did a dinner show each night for three nights. People loved the show, they came from all over Nevada and Utah and I was told even some folks came down from Canada. This proved to be one of the last major engagements we were to do as a team.

Stuart was diagnosed with a brain tumor. He spent a short time in the Santa Monica hospital, where he passed away on March 18, 1989. Suzy, Veeva and Lisa were at his side.

Stuart Hamblen, a great show business icon, had left us, but he left us with his great music and memories of a great father, husband and one of the best friends I ever had.

STUART HAMBLEN – FILMOGRAPHY

The Arizona Kid 1939

Carson City Cyclone 1943

Flame of Barbary Coast 1945

In Old Monterey 1939

King of the Cowboys 1943

King of the Forest Rangers 1946

Plainsman and the Lady 1946

The Savage Horde 1950

The Sombrero Kid 1942

Springtime in the Rockies 1937

STUART HAMBLEN MUSIC ALBUMS

It Is No Secret

Spell of the Yukon

Beyond the Sun

I Believe

The Cowboy Church

Of God I Sing

Remember Me

This Ole House

Worlds of Stuart Hamblen Vol. 1 thru 4

Suzy Hamblen Sings Vol. 5

The Man and His Music

World of Stuart Hamblen

CD

Stuart Hamblen Old Glory

PARTIAL LIST – STUART HAMBLEN'S SONGS

Don't Send Those Kids to Sunday School

Few Things to Remember

Gathering Home

Go on By

He Bought My Soul at Calvary

His Hands

How Big is God

I Believe

Is He Satisfied

It Is No Secret

It's a Brand New Day

I've Got So Many Million Years

My Religion's Not Old-Fashioned

Of God I Sing

Open Up Your Heart (And Let the Sunshine In)

Somewhere Beyond the Sun

Teach Me Lord to Wait

This Ship of Mine

Tho' Autumns Coming On

Until Then

What Can I Do for My Country

A MAN & HIS MUSIC

1974, LAMB & LION, STEREO-LLC-4001

Songs include:

Remember Me	2:47
This Ole House	2:49
My Mary	3:07
Late at Night	2:16
Texas Plains	2:51
It Is No Secret	2:57
Rack Up the Balls	2:44
Golden River	2:16
Little Old Rag Doll	2:44
Goodnight, Mrs. Jones	2:31
That's Just Livin'	2:14
Until Then	4:36

This is the album Stuart recorded in Nashville, 1973

CHAPTER 6

DALE EVANS

The Queen of the West, First Lady of western films, an ultimate professional, unlimited talents, one of the nicest people I've ever known, and my dear friend and client.

Remember the beautiful young lady I had seen in the movie *Swing Your Partner* in 1943, Dale Evans? Well, I instantly became a huge fan of Dale's. This was in an era when our top female stars were Lana Turner, Betty Grable, Rita Hayworth, etc. I think a lot of young boys were probably very smitten with these beautiful ladies, childhood crushes perhaps, but Dale Evans became my favorite. I was soon collecting photos, articles and news clippings on this new star.

Dale was born Lucille Wood Smith to Walter and Betty Sue Smith in Uvalde, Texas, on October 31, 1912. Her name was changed in infancy to Frances Octavia Smith. Her mother said Dale was a very outgoing child and first showed her drive to perform at the age of three when she tried to sing a gospel song in front of the members of her church. At the age of seven, Dale and her parents moved to Osceola, Arkansas, where she attended school. She was a very bright student and by the age of 12, Dale advanced to the ninth grade.

When Dale became 14, she was very smitten with a fellow student, Thomas Fox. They were very young, but they fell in love and she eloped with Thomas during her 14th year. By the time Dale was 15, she was pregnant with her son, Tom Fox, Jr. Happiness was short lived as Tom, Sr. asked Dale for a divorce before Dale was 16 years old. After they were divorced, Dale found herself alone with a small child to support. She enrolled in business school and got a job with an insurance company, which necessitated her move to Memphis, Tennessee, as that is where the company was located. Dale told me she also worked for Goodyear Tire Company in Memphis.

Dale loved to sing and one day at work her boss overheard her singing at her desk. He thought she had a very pleasant voice and offered to let her perform on the radio, a program which they sponsored. Her performance was better than well received and it wasn't long until Dale was at the top of the Memphis radio scene. She had jobs at local stations WMC and WREC in Memphis.

At around 19 years of age, Dale moved to Louisville, Kentucky and landed a job at WHAS Radio. WHAS was to be a huge milestone in her life. Initially, she began singing on WHAS as Frances Fox, her married name. Later she changed her name to Marian Lee. One day the station manager, Joe Eaton, felt that her name, Marian Lee, did not fit her well. He informed her he was changing her name to Dale Evans. She protested why, that's a boy's name. Joe told her he was a big admirer of

Dale Winter, an actress of the silent film era. The surname Evans came about as Eaton felt it was a good name for the announcer to say. So, Frances Fox became Dale Evans, a name the world over would one day know.

To show you how ironic life is sometimes, in the 1950s I was a manager for a local finance company in Indianapolis. One of our employees was the ex-wife of one Joe Eaton; the very same Joe Eaton that had given Dale Evans her name some years earlier.

While in Louisville, her son Tommy became quite ill. Dale, afraid he might have contacted polio, moved back to her family's farm in Texas. She felt safer to be near her family and how Tommy loved that farm and the small-town life that went with it. Tommy soon was on the road to good health.

Dale knew she needed to find a job. She did not wish to let her parents support the two of them. It wasn't long before she landed a staff job on WFAA radio in Dallas as the band singer on a popular program called *The Early Birds*. On *The Early Birds*, Dale worked with Eddie Dunn and Jimmy Jeffries. She sang hit songs of the '30s. While working on WFAA in 1937, R. Dale Butts, a pianist and orchestral manager she had known and dated some in Louisville, came to play the piano and do arrangements for WFAA. They resumed their friendship and began to date again. Within a year Dale was Mrs. Dale Butts. She remained married until her divorce from Butts in 1946.

Dale not only was on radio, but she worked as a vocalist with the Big Bands. She sang with Herman Walman's Orchestra and later Anson Weeks.

August 1938—*Rural Radio Magazine* pictured Dale on their cover. Dale posed on the bank of Turtle Creek in Dallas. It was a publicity shot for WFAA.

After two more years in Dallas, Mr. & Mrs. Butts moved to Chicago, Illinois, home of great music and talented bands. Dale soon landed a job as a jazz singer with an orchestra at the famous Edgewater Beach Hotel in their main showroom. Anson Weeks and his orchestra were playing at the Aragon Ballroom and were looking to hire a female vocalist. Dale auditioned and was hired. The next year Dale was traveling with the band on one-nighters and hotel engagements.

Dale learned that there was an opening on the staff at WBBM radio (CBS network). Again, an audition and Dale was hired.

At WBBM, she did six regular shows a week. All radio shows were done live in those days. Better be prepared. Dale was.

In 1940 Dale did a show for CBS called *That Gal from Texas*. She sang, talked and announced her own songs. While doing her radio shows, Dale was singing every night at the Blackstone, Sherman or Drake Hotels. Her efforts were paying off; she reached the top spot in Chicago, the Chez Paree Supper Club. She was on the same bill at the Chez with Ray Bolger (the famous dancer and one of the stars of MGM's *The Wizard of Oz* with Judy Garland) and Ethel Shutta. Dale felt she wasn't doing well and discussed her concerns with Ray Bolger. He suggested Dale sing one of her own compositions, "Will You Marry Me, Mr. Laramie?" That night she went on the stage and sang her song. She and the song were big hits.

Things were going very well for Dale. Life seemed good for her, Tommy and her husband. One day, Dale received an unexpected telegram that would change the course of her life forever. Joe Rivkin, a Hollywood agent (who I knew later in my career), had heard Dale sing on the radio. He wanted to see photographs of Dale with the idea of a screen test. Dale had no desire to be in films, she wasn't an actress and wasn't sure she was pretty enough to be in the movies. She paid no attention to that telegram, but more were to follow. Finally, Dale spoke to her program director and he suggested she play along and see what happened.

She was flown to Hollywood. Joe had set a screen test at Paramount for her; she was to test for *Holiday Inn*, starring Bing Crosby and Fred Astaire.

When the studio realized that Dale was not a dancer, at least not good enough to dance with Fred Astaire, she was disqualified. The studio, however, did a screen test. Her screen test was made with Macdonald Carey (*Days of Our Lives*). The test finished, Dale returned to Chicago to wait for the results. Dale told me she always wanted to be on Broadway, not movies. She was a big fan of Mary Martin, who was one of Broadway's brightest stars.

Soon, the call came from Hollywood. Paramount did not want the option on Dale, but 20th Century-Fox wanted to sign her to a one-year contract, her salary would be $400 a week. Dale had known what lean years were like, so $400 seemed like a lot of money. She and her family discussed the pros and cons and decided the answer would be yes.

In due time, Fox put Dale in two minor parts, *Orchestra Wives* with Glenn Miller and *Girl Trouble* with Don Ameche and Joan Bennett. Dale soon got over her initial reservations about film work. Fox was putting her in a starring role in a musical, *Campus in the Clouds*. But this was not to be, World War II had broken out. Soon, the Hollywood Victory Committee called and asked Dale to entertain troops at USO shows. Together, Dale and her husband entertained the troops at various camps. She sang, he accompanied her on the piano. Soon, they went their separate ways and saw less and less of each other. Shortly, the year at Fox was over and Dale's contract would not be renewed.

She asked Joe Rivkin to suggest an agent who could help her get back in radio. He suggested she meet with a fellow agent, Art Rush. (Art and I would become very good friends.) Art sent her to NBC, where they were auditioning for *The Chase & Sanborn Hour*, starring Edgar Bergen (actress Candice Bergen's father) and Charlie McCarthy. She landed the job and was a vocalist on the show and had some cute talk with Charlie for 43 weeks.

It was wartime and Dale did almost six hundred shows for the USO and the Hollywood Victory Committee. One of the shows was at Edwards Air Force Base in California. Edwards is located approximately 35 miles from where I currently live. At this show, she met a fellow performer on the bill. His name? Roy Rogers. (This was several years before she became Mrs. Roy Rogers.) They were not to meet again until she was signed to be his co-star in *Cowboy and the Senorita* at Republic.

Art Rush was Roy's agent and manager. Dale learned he was leaving for New York City to spend time with a star that already had made it! Roy was now "King of the Cowboys" and was very big in pictures. Dale exploded since Art obviously did not have enough time for both of them. She needed to find a new agent who could devote more time on her career. She left Art and signed with agent Danny Winkler.

Danny sold Republic Studios (Roy's studio) on signing Dale on a one-year contract. Dale was to remain with Republic for over eight years. After a short two weeks after signing her contract with Republic, she started work on her first film, *Swing Your Partner*, with Lulubelle & Scotty, a popular man and wife music team of that day. Remember? This was my first introduction to Dale Evans.

During this year at Republic, Dale would continue touring various Army bases. After the first year, Dale would continue under contract to Republic. One day Herbert J. Yates, the boss at Republic (I met Mr. Yates in 1962 and several times after that), called Dale up to the front office. He had seen the musical *Oklahoma!* and wanted to apply the same treatment to a new kind of Western. He wanted Dale as leading lady; the male star would be Roy Rogers. Dale wasn't too sure about this part; after all, she still wanted to do a big sophisticated musical. Mr. Yates assured Dale that she was perfect to co-star with Roy in this film. The film was *Cowboy and the Senorita*. The film was made and when it was released in 1944, Roy & Dale were an instant team. While at Republic, the two did 29 films. The first film, *Cowboy and the Senorita*, was in 1944, and their last film, *Pals of the Golden West*, was released in 1951.

In the 1940s, Dale ranked among the top Western stars in popularity, per the *Motion Picture Herald*, from 1947 to 1952. Dale ranked in the 8, 9 & 10th positions. Dale filmed 11 non-westerns at Republic.

From the beginning, Dale liked Roy. There was nothing phony about him. He dared be himself. He was extremely easy to be around. Ellie and I found Roy to be this way throughout the 40 years we were friends. On or off screen he was the same.

Dale was so successful in Roy's pictures that in 1946 columnist Erskine Johnson proclaimed Dale "Queen of the West." Dale continued her climb to success while her husband was also very busy on staff at Republic as an arranger. Dale Butts was a fine, talented man.

His life took different hours, etc., than Dale's. Many mornings she rose at 4:30 A.M. and went to the studio and worked until seven or 8:00 P.M. They grew apart and, in 1946, they were divorced. Although divorced, the two Dales remained very good friends.

About the time Dale was divorced from Butts, Roy was struck by tragedy. His wife Arlene Wilkins had given birth to a baby boy. Roy and Arlene had two daughters already, Cheryl and Linda Lou, so Roy was overjoyed that now they had a son. They named the child Roy Rogers, Jr. Eight days after giving birth, Arlene developed a blood clot and died. Roy was heartbroken. Roy & Dale continued to work most of their waking hours. They had a rapport, born of years of struggle. They also spent time together away from the studio. Dale got to know the children and they liked her.

Late in the fall of 1947, Roy & Dale appeared in a rodeo at the Chicago Stadium. While sitting on their horses in the chutes, waiting to ride out into the arena, Roy questioned Dale.

"What are you doing New Year's Eve?"

"I've no plans for New Year's Eve, it is so far off," replied Dale.

"Well, then, why don't we get married?" Roy asked.

As a youngster, Dale would dream that she would marry cowboy actor Tom Mix. She would see Tom and his horse in movies and all but worshipped them. Now the King himself was asking her to be Mrs. Roy Rogers. On the last day of 1947, Roy & Dale became husband and wife at the Flying L Ranch, home of Bill & Alice Likens, near Oklahoma City. They were wed at 5:00 P.M. by Rev. Bill Alexander. Roy's best man was his agent Art Rush, Dale's matron of honor was Mary Jo Rush (Art's wife). Also attending was Dale's parents, aunts, her son Tom and Tom's girlfriend, and later wife, Barbara.

Back home in Hollywood, Herbert Yates, head of Republic, had a concern that Dale would no longer be accepted by the fans, now that she was Mrs. Roy Rogers. Dale was out of Roy's pictures and did two dramas for Republic instead, starring in *The Trespasser* and *Slippy McGee*. The fans cried out that they wanted their "Queen of the West" back in Roy's movies. So, Dale returned as Roy's co-star in 1949 in the film *Susanna Pass*. Also, in the late '40s early '50s, Dale had her own weekly radio show on the Mutual Broadcasting System. She played the top 10 country hits and sang just two numbers each week. The show was called *Your Western Hit Revue*.

In December 1949, Dale learned that she and Roy were to have a child. Two months into the pregnancy, Dale contracted German measles. This would prove a threat to their baby. On August 26, Robin Elizabeth Rogers was born. They both were overjoyed, but only a short time as they were told she was a mongoloid. Even though very fragile, the Rogers chose to keep Robin at home. Home then was Encino, California. Her life was very short lived, but Robin blessed them in so many ways. Robin passed away. She was buried on her second birthday.

Later, Roy & Dale adopted Sandy as a playmate and chum for "Dusty," Roy, Jr. From Hope Cottage, they adopted Mary "Dodie" and in 1954, Roy & Dale traveled to Britain to appear with evangelist Billy Graham's London Crusade.

On a visit to Scotland they were introduced to an 11-year-old orphan, Marion (Mimi). Marion came home with them as a foster daughter. In 1955 the family grew again with the adoption of Debbie, a Korean orphan. Now there was Roy, Dale, Tom, Cheryl, Linda Lou, Dusty, Marion (Mimi), Dodie, Debbie & Sandy.

It is now 1956, and the Rogers have moved from Encino to Chatsworth, California. They have formed their own production company and produced the Roy Rogers half hour series. They continued to do recordings, television, rodeos and fairs.

Now, as fate would have it, in 1956 Don Davis, who was the publicist for the Indiana State Fair, somehow found out about my interest in Roy Rogers & Dale Evans and contacted me to do a scrapbook on Roy & Dale for the Riley Children's Hospital in Indianapolis. He would furnish photos, etc., and Ellie and I would compile the book. During their appearance at the fair, it was arranged that we would meet Roy & Dale backstage for a photo shoot and the next day we would visit Riley Hospital and present the scrapbook. Meeting Roy & Dale backstage was a lifetime event. Both were warm, friendly and we had photos taken, and visited with them for a short time. But it was a meeting we would never forget.

The next day, Ellie, Roy, Dale and I, accompanied by Art Rush (Roy's manager) and Mike North, their agent, visited the hospital and we presented the book. The folks at Riley were thrilled to see the King of the Cowboys and the Queen of the West in person.

We visited for a short time with the personnel at Riley Hospital, had some photos taken and then we left, as Roy & Dale had another show to do at the fairgrounds later in the day. I will always be grateful to Don Davis for the wonderful opportunity.

Now, moving forward to 1961, Ellie and I had moved to Sherman Oaks, California. One hot August day this same year we had gone to Canoga Park, about 9 miles from our home, to a record store to purchase a hard to find recording. Leaving the store, we encountered this lady wearing a red squaw dress and smiling as she came toward us. It was Dale and she remembered us from the Indiana State Fair. She was very warm and friendly and asked if we would join her at a nearby coffee shop for a soda or iced tea. Dale ordered cold buttermilk and we had iced tea. Dale explained that she and Roy lived only a few short miles from where we were and insisted we follow her to their ranch in

Chatsworth. We loved their huge sprawling ranch house of Spanish architecture. We saw Bullet, their dog, Trigger and the other horses in the stable. We stayed a short time and again we met their children.

That eventful day was to be the beginning of a 37-year friendship, until Roy's death in 1998. We remained like family (she referred to me as her baby brother) until her passing in 2001. We have known Roy, Dale and their family for over 45 years. During this time, we visited at each other's homes and truly became more like family than just friends. Their daughters, Dodie and Debbie, were frequent weekend guests at our home in Sherman Oaks and later at our home in Encino. The Rogers were a wonderful, loving family.

As I explained, they had lost their only natural daughter, Robin, in 1953 and Tom, Dale's son by a previous marriage, was now married and not at home. We shared so much; we were frequent guests at their TV tapings, live shows, etc.

One December day in the early '60s, Mimi, their daughter, phoned to see if Ellie & I could join the family and go out to Chatsworth and do some caroling for Dale & Roy. Yes, of course, we would be delighted to join in. So one cold December evening, we arranged to meet and motor back to the ranch. The drive after you left the main street was at least one mile long. We arrived, got out of our cars and gathered at the door and began to sing "Silent Night." Dale was the first to come to the door and very shortly was joined by Roy. We continued to sing and I remember the tears of joy in Dale's eyes and Roy was very moved. Both were so happy we cared enough to do this for just the two of them. We joined Roy & Dale in the house for refreshments and some great fellowship. It was a night that lives vividly in our memories. Thank you, Mimi, for organizing this memorable event. You are a dear lady and friend.

Another time Ellie and I recall, with pleasant memories, of Dale, is the day she phoned and wanted to invite us to a Hollywood Christian Group meeting. The Hollywood Christian Group was organized by those in the entertainment community who wished to express their Christian beliefs and their personal relationship with God. It was several members strong and they would meet on Monday nights at the Hollywood Knickerbocker Hotel.

Ellie and I both had been raised in the Church and we, of course, were anxious to learn more about this wonderful group of show people who believed as we did. So, we accepted Dale's invitation. Ellie invited Dale to our house in Encino for dinner and after dinner I drove Ellie, myself and Dale into Hollywood about 10 miles from our home. The meeting was everything we expected: Entertainers giving their personal testimonies and how they found God. Dale was a true woman of God. She was everything she claimed to be. The time we shared with Dale, Roy and the family enriched our lives and they were fun-filled events, happy and memorable.

We also shared their tragedies. I was one of the pallbearers at the funeral of their daughter Debbie, who was killed in a school bus accident, in 1964. She had gone with her church group to deliver clothes and food to a charity in Mexico. We were there when they lost son Sandy while stationed in Germany in 1966. Again, we attended another funeral. Sandy was out with some army buddies one evening and his buddies dared Sandy to drink up, "drink like a man," they chimed in. Sandy was young and should never have taken their dare, but accept the dare he did. It was wrong, very fatally wrong for him too. The next morning they found Sandy dead in his bunk. Too much alcohol for a boy that had never drank.

In the fall of 1966, Roy & Dale were to go to Vietnam to do shows for our servicemen. They stayed at the Meyer Kord Hotel in Saigon where the USO entertainers stayed. In fact, speaking recently to my friend, country/western recording artist Jim Case, he reminded me that he and his band were entertaining in Vietnam while Roy & Dale were there and they too stayed at the Meyer Kord Hotel. He recently shared with me a photo of himself and Dale & Roy, taken in Vietnam. But, through it all, Roy & Dale kept their faith and what inspiration they gave all who knew them.

In the early '60s, Roy & Dale moved to Apple Valley, California. As Dale told me many times, the house in Chatsworth held too many sad memories. We made the 112-mile trip to their home many weekends to visit.

Now I had my management company for about eight years and was doing very well. At dinner at Roy & Dale's one Sunday evening in 1970, Dale said, "How would you like to manage me?" Manage Dale? It would be like working with my sister. We talked about it and I said, "What about Art Rush?," who not only was Roy's personal manager, but Dale's agent. Dale said, "I'll take care of that," and so she did. She set a dinner meeting with me, Art, and herself at Alfonses Restaurant in Toluca Lake, California, near Art's office and down the street from NBC studios. She explained to Art that she wanted me to handle her for management, but we agreed Art would remain the agent.

Everything was fine, and Art and I, who had been friends for years, became even better friends. It worked well. Art passed away on New Year's Day, 1989. As Dale's personal manager, I worked with Art and others on behalf of her many TV, radio and personal appearances, both with Roy and on her own. I set many appearances for Dale: Dinah Shore's TV show, Merv Griffin, John Davidson's TV show, and local and national TV shows. I worked on behalf of her book publishing company, Fleming H. Revell, and publicity in newspapers, radio and TV. One major campaign I was involved in was the release of her book, *Woman*, in 1980.

As her manager I set interviews to promote both her books and recordings. One recorded album I recall was on the Word label, *The Heart of the Country*. I recall I set an interview with writer Claude Hall for *Billboard* magazine. Dale and I drove to Claude's office at *Billboard* and Claude did a very nice article. He remarked to Dale, "I wonder, Dale, if you are aware how much Dick cares about you and how very protective he is." She reached over, patted my hand, and said, "I sure do, Dick is more like my brother than my manager." A compliment like this doesn't come along in Hollywood often. God Bless Dale, she was the best. The cover for the album *The Heart of the Country* was shot by photographer Eric Skipsey, at Knottsberry Farm, with Dale standing on a table against a beautiful blue sky.

Dale recorded many albums from 1960 through 1980, including *It's Real, Country Dale*, and *Faith, Hope & Charity*. Books she wrote included *Angel Unaware*, about the death of Robin, *My Spiritual Diary, Hear the Children Crying* and *Only One Star*.

Leaving the office of *Billboard*, we were driving down Sunset Boulevard when Dale exclaimed, "Dick, what is that?" We were driving by a club named Filthy McNasty and in front of the club they had parked a hearse to advertise the club I suspect. Dale started laughing heartily and made the remark, "Well, I've seen it all!"

I recall when Dale's one-woman show was booked (she sang, gave her personal testimony and spoke of her career) at El Camino College, just south of Los Angeles.

Earlier that day we decided we would leave early and have dinner at Tony's on the Pier in Redondo Beach. Tony's is a very well-known seafood restaurant. We were seated near the waitress station and I felt we were being watched through a small round window. Finally, this waitress comes out to our table to get our food order. She kept looking at Dale and then at me as though she knew who we were. As Dale spoke to give her order, the waitress, with much certainty, said, "Do you know you sound just like Dale Evans?" Dale replied with a smile, "Yes, I do, I *am* Dale Evans." The waitress was so pleased she looked at me and I put up my right hand and said, "Yes, she is Dale Evans, but I'm not Roy Rogers." To this, we all laughed.

After we left the restaurant, we walked to the underground parking where my car was parked and proceeded to drive to El Camino College. Dale was more than on time, she was always punctual. About halfway through her program, Dale could see me backstage and I must have shown some concern and stress.

She mouthed to me, "What's wrong?"

After the program was finished and she came off stage, she exclaimed, "What's wrong?

"Dale, I must have left my wallet at Tony's."

"Let's go," she said, and we hurried back to the restaurant.

No one at the restaurant had seen my wallet, so back to the parking lot we headed and we both started searching the area where my car had originally been parked. Now, here is Dale, still dressed for the program, wearing a long ankle-length skirt and brown velvet blazer, down on her knees looking under cars to see if she can locate my wallet. No luck!

Driving back to the San Fernando Valley, my car started acting up, it just didn't seem like it was getting gas properly. My car was fairly new, a Lincoln Town Car.

We made it back to the Valley; I dropped Dale off and continued to drive home, about 4 miles away. When I got home, I told Ellie of my loss and, also, that the car was acting sluggish. Ellie said, "Give me the keys and let me look in the car," as to double check Dale and I. Shortly, she returned with my wallet in hand and said she had found it under the gas pedal of the car. So much for the car not running as well as it had been. I immediately phoned Dale, explained all was well, I had my wallet thanks to Ellie. She was very happy to hear the news.

I met one of Hollywood's most famous directors because of Dale. Director Norman Taurog (*Boys Town*, *Skippy*, *Mrs. O'Malley & Mr. Malone*, and several Elvis Presley films) worked tirelessly for the Braille Institute and one day he phoned me and said they were having a benefit show and they would love it if Dale would appear. On the specific date, Dale had a previous engagement, but I asked her if she could record a message that we could send to Norman. She went to the local radio station in Victorville, California near her and Roy's home in Apple Valley and recorded a very inspirational message for the Braille Institute. Norman was so pleased; he invited me to have lunch with him at the Friars Club in Hollywood. We had a wonderful lunch and a very nice visit. He was a very nice person.

One morning, Dale, Ellie and I were having breakfast at the Five Horsemen Restaurant in Toluca Lake, California. This man walked over to our table to say hello to Dale. They had known each other since their movie days at Republic Studios. Dale introduced us to David Sharpe, a very well-known stunt man. He had worked in a few of Roy & Dale's movies. We enjoyed speaking with him and found him to be polite and very nice. Republic had a lot of wonderful people on their lot.

In the 1980s, Roy decided he wanted to have that last big get together with his former friends from Republic. Roy & Dale invited most of the folks they had worked with, directors, producers, stars, grips, etc. Accepting Dale & Roy's invitations were director Bill Whitney, actress Adele Mara, cameraman Bud Thackery and oh so many people from the old days as Roy referred to them.

It was a warm, beautiful summer day in the high desert and the party was held on the Rogers' huge patio. Leaving the party, Adele Mara came up to me to ask me how to get back on the freeway that would take her back to Los Angeles. We told her to follow us to the freeway and she would be going in the right direction. Adele was a very nice woman. She was married to Roy Huggins, a producer at Universal Studios.

Shortly after the party, Bud Thackery gave me a beautiful picture of a painting of Dale that hung in a museum. It is a portrait of her in costume from the movie *Sunset in El Dorado*. Bud passed away on July 15, 1990. What a nice gentleman. His son Frank Thackery, a well-known director on television, is married to a Baxter, no relation as far as I know. Bud was a cinematographer on Dale's movies *Swing Your Partner* and *Here Comes Elmer*. He also worked on Roy's film *Son of the Pioneers* in 1942 and *King of the Forest Rangers* in 1946 with Stuart Hamblen.

Dale continued to write books, record gospel music, we did lots of television, local broadcast and national television.

One day in the 1970s, Dale phoned me and asked if I would come up to Apple Valley to hear their son Dusty (Roy Rogers, Jr.) and his new group. She wanted to help them get a manager. I agreed, of course, and I had first met Dusty when he was 10 years old. Ellie and I took a drive up to Apple Valley. We would have a nice visit with Roy & Dale and I would listen to Dusty and his new group. Dusty had put together a nice group of musicians and I could tell they had rehearsed a lot for their audition with me. I was blown away with what I had heard, and Dusty was in very good voice. He has a nice easy style. I was sure I could make good contacts and we should do very well as a team.

Dusty and his wife Linda invited us over to their home, which was located about 2 miles from Roy & Dale's home. We talked about what I thought his prospects would be and it was mutually agreed on our handshake that I indeed would take Dusty and his group as new clients. Again, it would be like representing family.

That evening we stayed for a short visit and shared our enthusiasm for the future. Ellie and I cared for Dusty and his family very much. Linda and I could make each other laugh over the smallest thing. Linda and Dusty have always been thought of by us as our own extended family. Dusty and Linda had three small children, Dustin (D.J.), Kelly and Shauna. They all look very much like their mother and dad.

On my return to Los Angeles, the next morning, I set in motion a program to get my new client off and running. First piece of business was how would I represent Dusty? He was born Roy Rogers, Jr., and Dusty was a nickname that his father gave him. I was still his mother's manager, what kind of conflicts were there to be? Between Dusty and I, we agreed that his stage name would be Roy "Dusty" Rogers, Jr. Now that the name was settled, I could proceed being his manager.

Second piece of business was to try and get Dusty a recording deal. Without a recording deal, I knew the bookings would be very difficult to obtain. This was the era in the late '70s when Nashville and recording companies seemed to be only interested in young artists that sang and wrote their own material. I approached a few people at some of the major labels, but seemed to be hitting a dead end. I was very protective of Dusty and I stood firm against those who would exploit him only because he was the son of two of the most famous stars of our time. I wanted to promote Dusty on his own abilities as a fine singer and entertainer.

I was in the office of my friend, Pete Korelich at Anahauc Records, the same company my client, Anacani, recorded for. Pete and I discussed Dusty and Pete reminded me they had a record label Vistone, which was country and pop. Pete and I would come together and do an album of Dusty, so a recording deal was made. Songs were selected, musicians, including Dusty's own group "The Highriders," and a studio was selected.

We would record at Hollywood's Sage & Sound studios on Sunset Boulevard. Pete was the producer and I was the co-producer. We had Jim Mooney as our engineer. The songs recorded on the album were "Tomorrow's Just Another Hope Away," "Cherokee Fiddle," "Beyond My Reach," "Workin' with a Five Piece Band," and six others.

We worked at the studio day and night, some nights as late as one or 2:00 A.M. Dusty and his group were very professional and wanted to get the best sound. Finally, the album is finished. Now I must decide on the album cover. I had my dear friend Bob Bucher take the photos for the art work. Bob had photographed many of the stars, as he had been on staff as a photographer for CBS in Hollywood. He also did most of my clients' publicity photos.

The photography session went well; we got very fine photos of Dusty. After Dusty and I selected the photos we particularly liked, the album was on its way to being available on the market. We finished the album on January 4, 1982. As this was Dusty's premier album, it was named *Just Call Me Dusty*, Roy "Dusty" Rogers, Jr. It was Vistone Records' number V1-656 with a great photo of Dusty, wearing a beige western shirt with an emblem of an American eagle, on the cover. Back cover had photos of Dusty and his group, The Highriders.

With the album finished, we did several radio shows to promote the product. One program I particularly remember was with Los Angeles station KLAC's DJ, Sammy Jackson. Sammy also had done liner notes for the album. Now I was beginning to set dates for Dusty and his group.

One of the early engagements was at The Horn, a nightspot in Santa Monica, California. This is the same club where so many stars had been discovered, stars like Jim Nabors. The Horn was not known as a country/western club and I wasn't sure I was making the right decision to book Dusty there. But, after all, this was a big "in" spot in Los Angeles during the 1970s and it should be a big deal for the owner of the club and Dusty.

The night of the show, I was overjoyed, Dusty had filled the place and people were still trying to get in. Had they all come out of curiosity to see this famous son of Roy & Dale's? If so, they soon found out that Dusty was his own person, and he did a terrific show.

New fans were born that night, Dusty was beginning to have a following and I was able to find a lot of work for him. His group played at Knottsberry Farm, Mid-Winter Fair, Date Festival, Orange County Fair and several venues in and around California. One place in particular was the Rio Nido Lodge above Santa Rosa on the Russian River. When I had been there earlier with clients, it felt like we were in the mountains. I explained to Dusty that the group would be playing in the mountains. He seemed excited. So in the summer of 1981, upon our arrival at the Rio Nido Lodge, he found out we were only a few feet above sea level. I was the joke of the day. Dusty and the group had their fun for the day. They loved performing in the *mountain* area. Several other club dates, fairs and festivals followed. I felt Dusty was doing well and it was time to reach out to Reno, Tahoe and the Las Vegas areas to test the waters.

On April 11, 1981, I had an appointment to see Gary LeMasters (now part of the Sons of the Pioneers), the talent buyer for Sam's Town Hotel & Casino in Las Vegas. Together, we negotiated a deal for Dusty and his group to appear there on May 29-30 & 31. They did two one-hour shows daily. They filled the showroom nightly. I had negotiated that the marquee was to have large point letters to advertise that Dusty was playing there.

Dale & Roy drove up to Vegas from their home in Apple Valley for Dusty's opening night. Driving down Tropicana Boulevard and turning onto Boulder Highway, where Sam's Town is located, Roy saw how large Dusty's name appeared on the marquee and when I met with them, Roy said, "Richard [he called me Richard for all the years we were friends], I never had my name in such bright lights as you have for Dusty and certainly not early in my career." (Of course he had, he just wanted to razz me.) He was one proud papa. Dusty and his group were booked once again and did well for Sam's Town.

Back to Los Angeles and more shows at venues in Southern California. In early 1982 the group played at George Air Force Base, in Victorville, for their Vegas night for the servicemen's wives.

In 1983 there was a Santa's Village in the San Bernardino Mountains, the Holiday Inn in Victorville and then on March 9, 1983, to Hawaii to do shows on the Kona Coast with his mom and dad. Roy, Dale, with Dusty and his group, would do shows at the Sheraton Hotel on March 10, 11, 12 & 13, 1983.

When we arrived at the Honolulu Airport, it got a little chaotic. Dale, Roy, Dusty and the four band members and Ellie and myself was a lot to look out for and we all must be together in a short while to board the flight to Kona. I needed to go through the security gate more than once and I was wearing a large silver western buckle on my belt. So, every time the alarm sounded, off would come the buckle. Finally, my last time I needed to go through the gate, a very nice Hawaiian lady, a security officer said, "Oh, honey, I know you by now and anyone that is Dale Evans' manager is okay in my book! Go on through." Times were remarkably different back then! We loved Kona, and we did some sightseeing while we were there and had a wonderful time.

Upon our return to Los Angeles, I had set a deal for Dale to do some voice recordings for a company that also would do some recordings with Pat Boone, Shirley Jones and Tommy Lasardo. Dale did a series called *Biblical Moments with Dale Evans*. I never saw a performer work so hard. She was absolutely wonderful. The tapes were recorded in Hollywood, and each day (we worked on this project about six weeks) I would ask Dale where she would like to have lunch. It was always the Tick Tock restaurant in Hollywood. The Tick Tock restaurant was a landmark, good food and a very comfortable (almost like dining at home) dĭcor.

One day, I remember these two ladies approaching our table. They asked if Dale would please sign their paper napkins. Dale answered, "I'll be happy to sign my autograph on something else, not on a paper napkin." They had paper in their purses and Dale very cordially gave them her autograph.

After the ladies had left our table, she said, "Dick, what on earth do they do with autographs?" Some folks thoroughly are thrilled to meet their favorite stars and cherish the autograph as a personal keepsake; others obtain autographs to sell to the highest bidder. I suspect the women truly loved meeting Dale and they would cherish this moment. Dale finished her recording and now it was time to get on with further business. During these tapings, Dale had introduced me to Shirley Jones, a nice lady.

During the early '80s, I had booked Dusty to perform at the horse show at Earl Warren Fair Grounds in Santa Barbara, California. Midway through the various horse exhibitions in Santa Barbara, Dusty and his group would perform a half-hour musical show for the audience. After their spot, the famous Montie Montana would do his show. To promote his appearance as well as the horse show, Dusty was advertised and interviewed by the local media, while appearing on an interview on local TV. Some folks from Regal Books in the neighboring town of Ventura caught the show. They contacted me and asked if we were interested in a book deal on Dusty's life? I spoke to Dusty and he liked the idea, so a contract was negotiated and was signed. The book, *Growing Up With Roy & Dale*, was published in 1986. Many shows followed, which include TV appearances on John Davidson's show, Dinah Shore, and *Christmas in the Barrio* on Spanish TV.

During the early '80s, Roy, Dale, Dusty and the Pioneers were booked to do three shows a day for three days over the Labor Day weekend at Knottsberry Farm in the John Wayne Theater. Now Labor Day weekend is a big deal. People come from all over.

Roy & Dale had appeared there before and still maintained their attendance records. It was a rather grueling weekend. Three shows a day is a lot, but we had wonderful crowds and the TV show *Entertainment Tonight* was in its infancy and they called and requested to come down to Buena Park, where Knottsberry is located, to interview the Rogers and do a short film for their TV show. The interview went well and they also covered the Labor Day Parade around the park with Dale, Roy & Dusty.

One bit of unexpected excitement that weekend was that Dusty & Linda's son Dustin (D.J.) fell at the pool where we were staying and hit his head. We rushed him to emergency, but he was absolutely okay. D.J.

was a tough little guy. Soon the holiday weekend came to a close and once again they had proved how beloved they were.

In 1983, Roy was booked to do a *Fall Guy* episode at 20th Century-Fox. The series was on ABC-TV and starred Lee Majors. The first episode was called "Happy Trails." It was episode #34 in season two of the series. Dusty guest starred and played an officer. It aired for the first time on January 12, 1983. Again in 1984, Roy & Dusty were on *Fall Guy*, episode #65, season #3. The episode was called "King of the Cowboys," airing on Wednesday, February 29, 1984.

In the early '80s I made a deal for Dusty and the group to appear in the main showroom at Cactus Pete's Hotel & Casino in Jackpot, Nevada near the Idaho border. I few from Los Angeles Airport into Salt Lake City, Utah and then and there I connected with a commuter flight that took me to Twin Falls, Idaho and then I took a rental car and made the drive down to Jackpot. And you thought show business was easy and glamorous! It took a lot of traveling and hard work to be on time for the next show. I made the flight to Salt Lake City without incident, but the twin prop plane I took to complete my journey was something else! I and another young male passenger traveling on business from Nashville were the only passengers. It was a bumpy, rough ride all the way to Twin Falls. The young man was not at all a seasoned flyer. He was very tense and, I'm sure, a little, no, *a lot* concerned. But, with a good pilot, we made the trip safely.

Dale had no engagement this date, so decided she would fly into Twin Falls and catch Dusty's opening show at Jackpot. She and a friend flew in later that day and when she met me at the hotel, she asked if I took the commuter flight out of Salt Lake. I answered indeed I had. Dale exclaimed, "WOW, what a ride!" It was a real vomit comet. Dusty's opening show went real well that night and Dale and I could forget the ride we had taken earlier in the day! Ah yes, show business!

Also, in the early '80s, I made a deal for Roy, Dale & Dusty to record an album together. It was a dream of mine for a long time. It was no problem with Dale & Dusty, after all I was their manager, but I needed to speak to Roy. Roy was very willing to join them on a recording and liked the idea. Like always, songs were selected for all three and I wanted Dale to record a few Big Band numbers. They would also record a Christmas medley. This album is a true collector's item. Roy, Dale & Dusty recorded some tracks at Capital Records in Hollywood, the same studio where Frank Sinatra and other top stars of the day had recorded.

Dusty and I flew to Nashville to record some of his songs to get that country sound. He recorded at the Reflections Studio. Then, back to Los Angeles shortly before Thanksgiving, 1982. Dusty and I had a stopover in Dallas/Ft. Worth Airport. There was a threat of a bad storm, maybe even a tornado. We sat on the plane, while the storm moved over the Dallas area. Now, as I explained, this is a few days before Thanksgiving, so this huge 747 plane was filled to capacity. Even with so many people aboard, the plane moved from side to side when the eye of the storm moved over us. Soon the weather cleared and we were on our way home. Home Sweet Home! Back home, we finished the album. We titled the album *Many Happy Trails*. It is a two-record set. A section of this book shares with you the album information.

The years I managed Dale & Dusty I will forever cherish. Writing this book, I look back and wonder how I did so much. I have only hit some of the highlights of my 37-year career. But like all wonderful events in our lives, they come and go. The mid-'80s saw me cutting back on my work and Dale was slowing down and Dusty and I agreed we had had a good run!

I will forever love the Rogers as my own and I speak with Dusty and his wife Linda from time to time. Dusty is very busy, along with his family, handling the affairs of the Roy Rogers-Dale Evans Museum, where he does two shows a day in his showroom in Branson, Missouri. While writing this book, on one occasion when I spoke to Linda, I reminded her that the best vegetable burrito I ever had was made by her two hands. Thanks, Linda, for the memory.

We have so many memories of the Rogers family and Ellie & I cherish each and every one of them.

CI News

Dale Evans: A Tribute

by Dick Baxter

On February 7, 2001, the entertainment world lost one of its brightest, gifted and most enduring stars, Dale Evans. With her passing, we also have lost a dear friend. In fact, the world has lost a beloved lady, a legend and an American icon.

My wife, Ellie, and I have been personal friends of Dale (Queen of the West) and her husband Roy Rogers (King of the Cowboys) whom we lost in July, 1998, and their family for over 45 years. What a special gift and honor!

Dale's passing on February 7th has left me with a huge feeling of loss and yet, my life has been richer, fuller and more rewarding for knowing Dale all these many years. We shared many joys, tears and laughter, especially during the time Dale was a client of mine. I recall many wonderful, and sometimes funny, situations with Dale. One I will share with you now.

Back in the 1970's, Dale was booked to do her one-woman show at El Camino College near Los Angeles. We decided we would leave early and stop and have dinner at Tony's on the pier in Redondo Beach. After our dinner, we drove on to the college where her performance was set to begin at 8pm.

During Dale's performance, she could see me standing in the wings, and she noticed that I was becoming somewhat upset. After she finished her show, she rushed up to me and asked, "What's wrong?" Since Dale was like an older sister to me, I appreciated her concern and explained that I had lost my wallet. At the same moment, we both realized that I must have dropped it in the underground parking area at Tony's. Together, we rushed back to the parking lot to find my wallet. Now, try to picture our beloved Dale, with full-length skirt, down on her knees looking under one parked car after another. Finally, she yells to me across the lot where I was searching some distance away, that she could not find said wallet.

We finally gave up and drove back to the San Fernando Valley some 60 miles away. After reaching home, I told my dear wife, Ellie, about my misfortune. Ellie, went out to our car and promptly located said wallet under the gas pedal of the car. Dale and I were so thankful, but soon we doubled up laughing as we thought of how we had gone searching, down on our hands and knees, all over Tony's parking lot.

This is only one of hundreds of incidents Dale and I shared over many years, and it was so typical of her. Always kind and helpful, she had gone to my aid without hesitation. And then when she learned of my little blunder, she was neither upset nor peevish. Instead, she responded to life's little difficulties with love and laughter.

I represented Dale as her manager for ten years. As a client, she was totally professional and most respectful. It was a joy.

Dale loved life and she truly loved the Lord. She had one of the hardiest laughs, and I will always cherish her sense of humor. When she walked into a room full of strangers, immediately her Texas "howdy" stole the hearts of all, and it was as if they had known her forever.

Dale was real. Nothing phony. Just a down to earth lady from Uvalde, Texas. She was a true champion, who acheived great sucess as a big

b a n
sing e
(Ans o
Week
Orchestr
in the 3
then beca
a   popul
actress, a
radio person
ity (Chase
Sanborn Ho
J i m m
Durante/Gar
Moore Show, et
She   was a
author (over
books),   recordi
artist and compos
("Happy Trails" a
"The Bible Tells M
So", etc.). Dale wou
have been a champi
no matter what care
choices she might ha
made.

She was a cari
and devoted wife a
mother. She and Roy ha
children, 15 grandch
dren, 36 great grandch
dren, and 6 great gre
grandchildren.

Dale Evans impacted the lives of everyo
around her in a very positive way. She and R
will live on in the hearts of their friends a
fans the world over.

I, along with my wife, Ellie, will alwa
remember our beloved friend, to whom
address one more expression of our friendshi
Rest in peace, dear friend, while we here, che
ish the many happy trails of memories you ha
left with us.

Roy & Dale Rogers
CI Photo Archive

Dale Evans Rogers

PHOTO COURTESY OF JENNIE KRO

TRIBUTE TO DALE EVANS BY DICK BAXTER
CLASSIC IMAGES – BOB KING

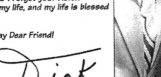

Page 20 Classic Images October 2003

Letter to a Friend

By Dick Baxter

Dear Dale:

How could anyone forget you and Roy? It is impossible for those of us who knew you for so many years. And, what about your devoted and loyal fans? You will live forever in their hearts.

Ellie, my wife, and I knew you and Roy for over 45 years. We were close friends and I was your personal manager from 1972 to 1984. What a pleasure and honor!

In remembering that this October 31st would be your birthday, I am recalling many wonderful times we shared. One of those times was in 1961. Ellie and I joined you and Roy for dinner at an Italian restaurant in Sherman Oaks, California. After dinner, as we were leaving the restaurant, I recall Roy being in a rather mellow and thoughtful mood. He patted me on the back and said, "Richard (he always called me Richard), as you go through life, if you are lucky to have just one loyal and devoted friend you can truly count on, then you will be a rich man."

Well today I am very fortunate to have many friends, but in recalling that evening in 1961, Dale, you truly must have been the one your husband was speaking of. You and Roy were certainly among our best friends for oh so many years.

Dale, there is hardly a day goes by that I don't think, I must call you about this or that. I miss all the work we did. Your recordings, new book releases, TV shows - Dinah Shore, John Davidson Show, Merv Griffin Show and numerous others.

Our home in California is at 4,400 ft. elevation and surrounded by the beautiful Tehachapi Mountains. As we leave our home for a trip to town or wherever we are going at the time, I see the beautiful haze on our mountains and I can almost hear you singing your beautiful composition "Hazy Mountains". Forget you? Never.

You will always be a part of my life, and my life is blessed because of you.

Happy Birthday Dear Friend!

Dick

Dale Evans, Queen of the West.

Long time manager Dick Baxter and client and friend Dale Evans in 1978.

TRIBUTE TO DALE EVANS BY DICK BAXTER
CLASSIC IMAGES – BOB KING

PERMISSION – A. JODY WILLIAMS, DETROIT FREE PRESS

ROY ROGERS-DALE EVANS
COLLECTORS ASSOCIATION
POST OFFICE BOX 1166
PORTSMOUTH, OHIO 45662

NANCY HORSLEY
EXECUTIVE SECRETARY

1820 HUTCHINS - PORTSMOUTH, OH 45662-3160
PHONE: (740) 353-0900   CELL: (740) 821-8943
E-MAIL: nancyandlarue@verizon.net
ourchurch.com/member/r/RRFestival-OHIO/

THE FILMS OF DALE EVANS

The Big Show-Off – 09/09/45

Casanova in Burlesque – 12/21/43

Girl Trouble – 10/09/42 – 20th Century-Fox

Here Comes Elmer – 10/05/43

Hitchhike to Happiness – 06/07/45

Hoosier Holiday – 08/19/43

In Old Oklahoma – 10/13/43
(War of the Wildcats)

Orchestra Wives – 09/04/42 – 20th Century-Fox

Slippy McGee – 01/07/48

Swing Your Partner – 05/11/43

The Trespasser – 07/15/47

The West Side Kid – 08/05/43

FILMS OF ROY ROGERS & DALE EVANS

Along the Navajo Trail – 03/46

Apache Rose – 02/17/47

Bells of Coronado – 01/08/50

Bells of Rosarita – 05/13/45

Bells of San Angelo – 05/07/47

Cowboy and the Senorita – 05/12/44

Don't Fence Me In – 10/11/45

Down Dakota Way – 09/08/49

The Golden Stallion – 10/28/49

Heldorado – 12/01/46

Home in Oklahoma – 11/12/46

Lights of Old Santa Fe – 11/06/44

Man from Oklahoma – 08/08/46

My Pal Trigger – 06/04/46

Out California Way (guest star) – 11/12/46

Pals of the Golden West – 11/15/51

Rainbow Over Texas – 04/18/46

Roll on Texas Moon – 09/02/46

San Fernando Valley – 09/15/44

Song of Arizona – 05/05/46

FILMS OF ROY ROGERS & DALE EVANS (cont.)

Song of Nevada – 08/05/44

South of Caliente – 10/15/51

Sunset in El Dorado – 09/29/45

Susanna Pass – 05/09/49

Trigger, Jr. – 06/30/50

Twilight in the Sierras – 03/22/50

Under Nevada Skies – 07/19/46

Utah – 03/08/45

The Yellow Rose of Texas – 06/24/44

(These are all Republic pictures)

ROY ROGERS TV SHOW

Premiered on NBC-TV–12/30/51 to 6/23/57

Sunday – 5:30 – 6:00 P.M. (CST)

Syndicated – 1958 –1964

The series starred Roy Rogers, Dale Evans, Pat Brady, Trigger, Bullet & Nellybelle the Jeep

BOOKS – DALE EVANS ROGERS

Angel Unaware – 1953

My Spiritual Diary – 1955

To My Son – 1957

Christmas is Always – 1958

No Two Ways About It! – 1963

Dearest Debbie – 1965

Time out Ladies – 1966

Salute to Sandy – 1967

The Woman at the Well – 1970

Dale, My Personal Picture Album – 1971

Cool It or Lose It! – 1972

Finding the Way – 1969

Where He Leads – 1974

Let Freedom Ring – 1975

Trials, Tears & Triumph – 1977

Hear the Children Crying – 1978

Woman – 1980

Grandparents Can – 1982

Let Us Love – 1982

God in Hard Times – 1984

The Home Stretch – 1986

BOOKS – DALE EVANS ROGERS (Cont.)

Only One Star – 1988

Say Yes to Tomorrow – 1993

In the Hands of the Potter – 1994

Our Values – 1997

Rainbow on a Hard Trail – 1999

PARTIAL LIST OF DALE EVANS' SONGS

Will You Marry Me, Mr. Laramie? – 1/8/40

The Little Fat Man with the Big White Beard – 12/11/40

My Heart is Down Texas Way – 4/18/41

I'm in Love with a Guy Who Flies in the Sky – 12/11/40

There's Only One You – 8/21/44

I Wish I Had Never Met Sunshine – 12/17/45

My Heart Went That-a-Way – 12/30/46

His Hat Cost More Than Mine – 11/3/47

Aha, San Antone – 3/1/48

Cowgirl Polka – 9/23/49

It's Saturday Night – 1949

Happy Trails – 10/26/51

Don't Ever Fall in Love with a Cowboy – 7/18/52

Hazy Mountains – 7/18/52

T for Texas – 7/18/52

The Bible Tells Me So – 2/3/55

Merry Christmas, My Darling – 5/5/67

Christmas is Always – 11/3/67

Angel Unaware – 2/26/75

The Heart of the Country – 2/26/75

Feeling Country Blue – 10/12/76

Jesus is my Closest Friend – 8/24/81

DALE EVANS FACTS

10/31/12 – 01/07/2001

UNDER REPUBLIC PICTURES CONTRACT

April 1943 thru December 1947

FINAL PICTURE @ REPUBLIC

Pals of the Golden West with Roy Rogers, 1951

POPULARITY RANKING BY
MOTION PICTURE HERALD

1947 – 9th place

1950 – 10th place

1951 – 9th place

1952 – 8th place

BOX OFFICE POLL

1951 – 5th place

1952 – 4th place

1953-1955 – 6th place

THE ROGERS SHOW – NBC-TV

1951 – 1957

STANDING TALL IN THE SHADOWS ✦ 135

DALE EVANS FACTS (Cont.)

MARRIAGE TO ROY ROGERS

December 31, 1947

HOLLYWOOD WALK OF FAME

Dale has two stars on the Hollywood Walk of Fame. One star is at 6638 Hollywood Blvd., and the second is located at 1737 Vine Street, across from the Capital Records Building

She joined her husband, Roy Rogers as Grand Marshalls of the Hollywood Christmas Lane Parade in 1981.

DUSTY'S FIRST ALBUM

Just Call Me Dusty

Roy "Dusty" Rogers, Jr., & The Highriders

LABEL: Vistone Records V1-656 LP

Date: 1982

Producer: Peter Korelich

Co-Producer: Dick Baxter

Recorded at: Sage & Sound Studios

Hollywood, California

LIST OF SONGS

Tomorrow's Just Another Hope Away

I Don't Want to Hear Another Love Song

How Could Anything So Wonderful Be So Wrong

Cherokee Fiddle

Beyond My Reach

Nora

Workin' with a Five Piece Band

Precious Sleep

Among My Souvenirs

You're the Song I Sing

DUSTY'S FIRST ALBUM (Cont.)

SINGLE – VISTONE V1-2091

How Do You Speak to an Angel?

B/W

No One Knows Better Than Me

CHAPTER 7

ANACANI

Talented, beautiful, a friend to Ellie and I and our family.
One of Lawrence Welk's brightest and best beloved stars.

WHILE IN LAS VEGAS IN THE EARLY '70S, I WAS WATCHING TV IN MY hotel room. Switching channels, I came across this beautiful young female singer and was totally enchanted by her looks and her beautiful voice. I was so impressed with this lovely lady, I do not recall what song she was singing, only that I thought she was great! The TV show was *The Lawrence Welk Show*, and this delightful young girl was Anacani. I immediately jotted down this information in my notebook and knew that on my return to Los Angeles I would seek out more information regarding this talented young lady.

Upon returning to my office in Los Angeles, I started doing my research on this great new talent with the idea that she may need a manager. First, I discovered that not only was she on the Welk show, but she was recording for the local-based Anahauc Records, Pete Korelich, and his partner Jaime De Aguinaga. We had a very nice telephone conversation. I learned from Pete and his partner Jaime that Anacani was new with their company and they had just released her first album (the self-titled *Anacani*). I also learned that Anacani did not have a personal manager. After hearing about my experience in the entertainment business, Pete wanted to set up a meeting with himself, Anacani and me. It was decided we would have a luncheon meeting at the Tail o' the Cock restaurant in Studio City. This was shortly after our phone conversation.

Joining us for our meeting would be Anacani's mother, Maria, as Anacani was not yet 18 years of age. Maria was a beautiful, very gracious lady. I liked her immediately. Anacani and I seemed to have never been strangers. We felt comfortable and we instantly liked each other. At that very first meeting I learned that Anacani was born Anacani Maria Consuelo Y Lopez Cantor Montoya on April 10, 1954 in Sinaloa, Mexico, the 6th of 7 children of Mexican and French parents. She had moved to the United States with her parents when she was a child. When she was still in middle school, she joined her parents in a trip back to Mexico and it was there that her singing talents were discovered by a TV producer. She appeared on Mexican television in various variety shows and did live concerts as well.

After completing high school in Los Angeles, she and her parents were visiting the Lawrence Welk Resort in Escondido, California, where she was discovered by Lawrence Welk, the bandleader, himself. She worked briefly at the resort and soon Mr. Welk invited her to perform on his weekly TV show. On January 1973, after a few more guest appearances, she was hired as a regular performer on the show. She now also toured with the Welk live shows and recorded an album, *Lawrence Welk presents Anacani*, through Ranwood Records.

As I have explained, our meeting that day went very well and Anacani became a "Dick Baxter Management" client, joining my roster of clients, Dale Evans and Stuart Hamblen. Anacani remained with me for about 8-9 years. During my time with her, she continued doing the Welk show and touring with the cast of the show. It was very difficult to try and work dates for Dick Baxter Management around her schedule with Welk, but Anacani was worth it. She was a delight to know and very professional for her young years. We did TV, live shows and also recording more for Pete at Anahauc Records.

I particularly remember a news photographer for the Mexican newspaper here in the U.S. as well as in Mexico and Latin America doing a photo layout on Anacani and me at the La Fonda Restaurant in downtown Los Angeles. He also had us go outside and took some more pictures. In one I pretended to hail a cab for Anacani. These were to be used to promote Anacani, and the photographer liked the idea of my being included. I never saw these photos as I guess they were printed in magazines and newspapers in Mexico and the Latin America countries.

Ellie and I had the honor to accompany her and her mother when she received several entertainment awards, as well as autograph parties for the release of her new albums.

In the late '70s, when she was appearing with the *Lawrence Welk Show* at the MGM Grand, Anacani treated Ellie and me to a very nice anniversary dinner. I believe it was mine and Ellie's 21st or 22nd anniversary.

As the years passed, she fell in love with Rudy Echhaverria, a fine young man, very bright and he could offer Anacani a very stable future. Anacani informed my wife, Ellie, backstage at a benefit show that I had booked her on, that she and Rudy would be getting married. All the single guys around the country, I'm sure, were heartbroken.

As a manager who had a very stable married life, I had to be all for this union. Anacani and Rudy were wed in August 1978, but a while before they were married Anacani and I had a mutual agreement to dissolve our business relationship. In the early '80s we mutually called it quits, but our friendship remained strong and healthy.

Ellie, Ellie's mother, sister and I loved Anacani. She meant a lot and still does to our family. Our friendship has remained strong and Anacani is like the daughter Ellie and I would have wanted had we had children.

Today, Anacani and Rudy have a lovely daughter, Priscilla, now in her 20s. Older than her mother was when she came to Dick Baxter Management.

She still performs all over the world, and is as beautiful as she was when I first saw her on that TV back in my room in Las Vegas many years ago. She's a great mother and wife. She and her family will always be dear to Ellie and me.

CHAPTER 8

JUNE WADE

She thought my phone call to her was a joke.

IN THE FALL OF 1973, A RECORD PRODUCER FROM OKLAHOMA PHONED me and asked if he could submit to me an album he had just recorded with a new gospel artist, June Wade. I explained that we were not taking on any new clients at this time. He would like to send me a copy of the album to get my opinion. I gave in and told him he could submit the album, but don't expect too much.

In a few days the album arrived, *Think on These* by June Wade. It took a few days, but the album was among some of the other material I wished to listen to. It was a Saturday, a day off for me, very rare to have the time to catch up on my mail. I put June Wade's album on the turntable, hit play, and soon I heard a most amazing voice. June sounded Country. A young Patsy Cline. When she sang "The King is Coming," I realized this was an artist I wanted to meet.

The producer had sent June's phone number along with the album just in case I should like to give her a call. He had the right intuition. I picked up my phone and began to dial the number. The area code was very familiar to me. I was calling June Wade in Apple Valley, California where my client Dale Evans lived. The phone rang and the voice at the other end said hello.

"Are you June Wade?" I inquired.

"Yes," the very pleasant voice replied.

"Well, this is Dick Baxter, Dale Evans and Stuart Hamblen's manager." (June later told me she thought my call was a joke and she wanted to reply, "Yes, and I'm Dale Evans.")

I explained to her that her new record company had submitted her album to me and I was blown away with her sound. We talked for a while; I learned she had been singing since her teens and that this was her first gospel album. She now was a married lady in her late 20s with two children. Did she know my client Dale? Everyone knows Roy Rogers & Dale Evans, she replied, but she had never met Dale, just had seen her around Apple Valley, although she had done a Christmas show nearby in Victorville and Roy Rogers was also featured on the program as well as country/western artist Billy Mize.

We made an appointment for me to drive up to her home the following weekend. The next weekend, on an early Saturday afternoon, Ellie and I arrived at June's home. We were met by a very pretty dark-haired lady. We are introduced to her family, which also included her father, who was staying with her for a while. It was easy to get to know June, she was very warm, personable and articulate. Our meeting that afternoon gave me the information about June's singing career to date. She started out in country music, singing gospel along the way, working mostly fairs, nightclubs and special events, all the time being a wife and raising her children. Being a Christian, June decided at this time in her life to devote her career to Christian music and to her Christian witnessing, singing in churches and Christian events around the country.

This would be fine with me, but I felt she was wrong not to continue in secular work. I explained, with my contacts and know-how, she could perform in Las Vegas, Reno, Tahoe and most venues that booked country artists.

We decided to give management a try. I had my concerns about her, though. How far could she go in the entertainment business without performing in the major venues I had in mind for her? I booked June on some local Christian TV stations. Glendale, California was the first one. Young football player Jack Youngblood was on the same program. June sang a couple of songs from her new album. She went over very well.

Next, she appeared on TBN in Orange County with Jim & Tammy Faye Bakker. (They were just getting a start in TV.) We did several TV shows and many churches around Southern California. June declined to accept any work in the secular field. Las Vegas and the likes were not of great interest to her. Her Christian faith was very important to her, and to me as well. But, many artists were doing secular work without jeopardizing their faith. In fact, I believed that Christians should sing to all people, wouldn't that be a ministry in itself to bring music to all! Many needed to hear this form of music.

June could have been a great country singer with a huge following, but, as I said, it wasn't in the cards.

After about a year, I knew I had brought June as far as I could without the ability of being able to go full blast with her career. A manager's hands were tied. We parted as manager and client in 1974, both realizing what we had done, what we set out to do, gave it a try.

Today, June and her husband Ken remain two of Ellie and my best friends. We speak on the phone and visit often. June is one of the dearest ladies I have known and she is truly the lady that should have been a star.

If you had been lucky enough to have heard her sing in those days, I'm sure you would agree!

CHAPTER 9

PEGGY COBURN

Beautiful Voice

Beautiful Spirit

Beautiful Lady

WHAT CAN I SAY ABOUT PEGGY COBURN, ONE OF OUR DEAREST AND longtime friends! She was represented by me as her personal manager only a short time, about three years, but she was truly a professional and great to work with.

Peggy was born in Clearfield, Pennsylvania, on July 13, 1922, as Peggy Irene Watson, and, spent her childhood in Western Pennsylvania except for a few years that her family lived in Chelsea, Massachusetts. She lived there from age 3-6 years of age. Her father, Leslie E. Watson, and mother, Edna, were involved with the Salvation Army as Senior Majors. She began her musical career singing with the Salvation Army band. A famous voice coach heard Peggy sing and offered her a three-year scholarship in her last three years of high school. This led to a full scholarship with the Julliard School of Music in New York.

Upon completion of her studies, which included opera, Peggy began to find professional singing jobs around New York City. While in New York, she worked in back-up groups for Arthur Godfrey of TV fame, Kate Smith, Perry Como, and many others.

She married musician Bill Coburn in 1949 and they moved to California in 1955. Together they worked throughout the United States and Europe. Peggy sang and Bill was her pianist/composer. A son, Spark, was born to Bill and Peggy in 1954.

Peggy, who has a rare voice, one of the very few, true, contraltos in existence, has sung in many parts of the world. Her concerts have taken her throughout the United States, Great Britain and the Far East, including Japan, Korea and the Philippines. One of her British tours culminated in her appearance as soloist for the famed Christmas Festival at Usher Hall in Edinburgh, Scotland. Other venues for Peggy have been Carnegie Hall, New York City, Constitution Hall, and Washington, D.C.

During the busiest of years, Peggy managed to record several LP albums, such favorites as *Hymns to Your Heart*, *Sing A-Ho*, *10,000 Angels* and *The Master is Coming*.

In the early '70s, a friend of Dale Evans', also a very good friend of Peggy's, called my office regarding Peggy. She was looking for a manager and would I please meet with her and hear her sing. I agreed. Meeting Peggy was like meeting someone from home. Very pleasant, cordial and she showed tremendous enthusiasm, and what a beautiful voice, and still is beautiful today. She was great to look at, beautiful red hair and gorgeous green eyes. She was truly an Irish colleen.

Peggy and I agreed to work together and for three years we did television shows, concerts, Hollywood Bowl (which she did several Easter Sunrise Services). Peggy had an opportunity to work in Canada and I felt I could not stand in her way. So, a dissolution of our relationship as client/manager came about. But, as I said, she has remained one of our dearest and most valued friends and they say clients don't like managers very well.

Peggy lost her dear husband Bill in 1985. She remains beautiful and in great spirits and now teaches music. We speak on the phone about 3-4 times a month and we look forward to our visits.

CHAPTER 10

CATHERINE McLEOD

A lovely, graceful and very talented actress.

WHEN WE LIVED IN SHERMAN OAKS, CALIFORNIA, I WAS CONSTANTLY running into actress Catherine McLeod at our various local shops. Catherine and her husband, actor Don Keefer (they married in 1950), lived near our home. We would speak and sometimes, take a moment to chat. We knew several people in common; Catherine knew Dale and Roy as she worked at Republic in the late 40s and well into the '50s. Catherine was always charming and very easy to speak with. She liked Ellie and me. I know she respected me as a manager, as I respected her as one of our very fine actresses.

Catherine was born July 2, 1921 in Santa Monica, California, of Scottish descent. In 1944 she began her film career in an uncredited part in the serial *The Tiger Woman*, followed by *The Thin Man Goes Home*, also an uncredited part. In 1946 she had the small role of Louise in MGM's *The Harvey Girls*, and a few other minor roles for MGM. In 1946 she was signed by Republic, where she received her greatest role, that of Myra Hassman, a concert pianist, in Frank Borzage's film *I've Always Loved You*.

During the next few years, Republic starred Catherine with Don Ameche in *That's My Man* and *The Fabulous Texan* and *Old Los Angeles*, both with William Elliott.

Catherine had a very active career in TV in the '50s and '60s: *The Virginian*, *Gunsmoke*, *Hawaiian Eye*, *Have Gun - Will Travel*, *General Electric Theater*, *Matinee Theater*, among many, many more.

As I explained earlier, Catherine and I had met several times and, in the early '70s, she approached me about management. I would give it a try. Catherine and I had good rapport. She was a professional and had done volumes of work. Still, Catherine was easy for me to represent. She listened. During her time with me, she was in three or four film projects. She played the Vogue Lady in 1976's *Lipstick*, with Anne Bancroft, Perry King and Chris Sarandon. During this time, she brought Chris Sarandon by my office to meet me.

She was also in the 1971 TV movie *Vanished*, in the role of Grace. We were client and manager for a very short time, but it was a pleasure working with this very capable actress.

She left acting, except she had a recurring role on NBC daytime drama *Days of Our Lives* and she wrote for a national soap opera magazine.

In 1991, as lovely and graceful as ever, she appeared as one of the interviewees on the 1990 two-hour TV documentary *The Republic Picture Story*. Catherine passed away on May 11, 1997 from pneumonia. Her husband, Don Keefer, sons John Keefer and Don, Jr., survive her.

Catherine is another who enriched my life by just knowing her and her family.

CHAPTER 11

HI BUSSE & THE FRONTIERSMEN & JOANIE

They called him Hi-Pockets. He stood tall and lean, a very gentle man.

Joanie, talented, very pretty, easy to work with and a dear friend right up to the present.

The group was similar to the Sons of the Pioneers, but with a lovely female member.

ONE DAY IN THE MID-'70S, MY PHONE RANG AND THE GENTLEMAN making the call wished to speak with Dick Baxter.

"Hello, I'm Dick Baxter," I answered.

The voice on the other end spoke with what I believed was a South Texas accent.

"I'm Hi Busse and Art Rush [Roy Rogers' longtime manager and my friend] gave me your number. I'm looking for a good personal manager and Art assured me that you were one of the best."

Art had explained to Hi that if I was taking on any new clients, he should try and convince me to sign him and his group, The Frontiersmen & Joanie. (More about Joanie later.)

Well, if my friend Art Rush recommended Hi, then, of course, I would invite him to my office for an interview. The day came for his interview; I immediately liked this very tall, lean cowboy. He was very articulate and very charming. But, I thought I was meeting another Texan, when, in fact, I learned that he was born in Warroad, Minnesota in 1914. He was born Enright August Busse. After establishing himself in the country/western business he was nicknamed Hi-Pockets by his peers.

Going back to 1934, he told me he had played accordion for Jack Dalton's Riders of the Purple Sage on KFI radio. He later joined the Texas Ramblers and the Saddle Tramps and in 1938 he founded the Frontiersmen. He and the group toured with Roy Rogers (wait a minute, I know that man) in Texas in 1938 after Roy's first film at Republic, *Under Western Stars*.

He and the group also worked with Rex Allen, Tex Ritter, Tex Williams and later Roy Rogers & Dale Evans & Dusty. He and the group also worked with Eddie Dean. In the early 1960s, he hired for the first time a female vocalist and musician, Joanie Hall. Now it was Hi, his guys and a female member. They still were similar to the Sons of the Pioneers, except with a big difference, Joanie. As Hi Busse & the Frontiersmen & Joanie, the group had done very well. They were doing concerts and fairs with the members of the *Bonanza* TV Show with Lorne Green and Michael Landon. They also worked with the *Gunsmoke* TV cast, James Arness, Dennis Weaver, Ken Curtis and Amanda Blake. I had met Amanda a few years back and she was one of my favorite people.

This interview was enough for me. Hi and his group were the right type of talent for me to manage. We agreed that day to become manager and client. I met the band members and Joanie and knew I had made a wise decision. I had never signed a group before, so this was somewhat a challenge for me.

Over the next few years, we did live shows, TV and various personal appearances. I also made a recording deal for them to record for Anahauc Records under the Vistone label. We cut their first recording at Sage & Sound in Hollywood where Dusty was also recording some of his material.

I'll never forget the deal I made for them with Knottsberry Farm. They would be riding the Knottsberry float New Year's Day, January 1, 1980. We had to be in Pasadena by 5:00 A.M. that morning. It was very cold and damp.

He had brought his motor home so we all had a place to keep warm for a while. Soon it was time for the Frontiersmen & Joanie to be positioned on the Knottsberry float and be in place for the parade to begin. However, this had to happen a good hour before the parade began. As I said, it was very cold, but soon the sun was up and it would be a beautiful day for the parade. The parade, as all previous parades, was beautiful and went off without a hitch. In spite of the early hour, and the extreme chill in the early morning air, I believe the Frontiersmen & Joanie felt this was a high point in their careers and felt very honored.

My friend, Rick Huff of the Western Music Association, and also host and producer of radio programs, knowing I was Dale's manager and I was putting on paper some of my Hollywood memories, wished to share the following:

"Hi Busse's association with Roy & Dale was long and love filled. Hi formed his Frontiersmen to back his friend Len Slye in his first public performance using the name 'Roy Rogers' (1938). Along with Ray Whitley, Hi & the Frontiersmen premiered the songs 'Along the Navajo Trail' and 'Don't Fence Me In' with Roy in Madison Square Garden (1945). Hi's Frontiersmen provided the musical support for Roy & Dale's network radio show in the period between Foy Willing and The Riders of the Purple Sage and Roy Lanham's Whippoorwills, and over the years they backed Roy & Dale at most shows not done by the Sons of the Pioneers."

The few years I represented the group we played many venues, fairs, rodeos, clubs, concerts, etc. Representing the Frontiersmen & Joanie was a career highlight for me.

CHAPTER 12

Joanie Hall

WHAT SET THE SONS OF THE PIONEERS AND THE FRONTIERSMEN APART was the very pretty and talented Joanie Hall.

Joanie got her career started by doing a lot of demo work and club dates, etc. In 1955, Woody Fleener had started the Sage & Sound record label in Hollywood. One of his first major vocalists he signed was cowboy star Eddie Dean. (In 1946 and 1947 he was voted among the ten best moneymaking stars in the *Motion Picture Herald* Fame poll. Eddie was born on July 9, 1907, in Posey, Texas.)

Also signed at the time was the Frontiersmen and Marian Hall (Joanie's sister), as a featured steel guitar player. Joanie would be called in to do a chorus or play rhythm guitar. But it wasn't long before she was noticed for her own talent.

Eddie Dean saw a lot of talent in Joanie and one day he called her to let her know he wanted to record a duet with her. They recorded "Open Up Your Door," backed with "Sign on the Door." After that recording, Woody Fleener signed her to her own recording contract. Joanie recorded "Jimmie Loves Jeanie Bee" and "Just Because." Both were *Billboard* pick hits and she continued to do personal appearances.

Hi Busse asked her to join him and the Frontiersmen, which consisted of Wayne West and Hal Southern in the early '70s. Joanie proved to be a big asset to the group. She was 5'9", blonde, with brown eyes and a voice so beautiful and soft and she could sing any part of harmony. Joanie also worked a lot on her own doing fairs, concerts, festivals, etc. Ellie and I loved Joanie and still do. We live about 150 miles apart, but speak often by phone and we share E-Mail. Joanie is a big part of our lives. Her warm, caring friendship has endured all these years. Thank you, Joanie, we love you.

When the group retired in the late '80s, so did Joanie. Joanie now lives near the ocean in Ventura, California.

CHAPTER 13

Gloria Jean

I MET GLORIA JEAN IN SHERMAN OAKS, CALIFORNIA IN THE SUMMER of 1963. I had an appointment with a business located on Ventura Boulevard and, making my entrance into the building, the first face I saw was Gloria. I instantly recognized her, the beautiful lady that had starred in many Universal Pictures: *The Under-Pup*, *If I Had My Way*, *Never Give a Sucker an Even Break* (with W. C. Fields, one of my favorite stars), *Mister Big*, *Get Hep to Love*, *Pardon My Rhythm*, *An Old-Fashioned Girl*, *Copacabana*, and many others, several of which I had seen in my teens.

I introduced myself and Gloria was very gracious and friendly. We spent a few minutes talking and realized we had many acquaintances and friends in common. That day began a longtime friendship between me, Ellie and Gloria's family.

We visited Gloria in her San Fernando Valley home soon after and met her family, her mother Eleanor and her son Angelo. Her sister Bonnie was not at home that day, but we later met Bonnie and she, too, has become a dear friend.

Gloria was born Gloria Schoonover on April 14, 1926 in Buffalo, New York to Eleanor and Ferman Harold Schoonover. She had three sisters, Sally born September 4, 1924, Lois born February 8, 1928 and a baby sister, Bonnie, born November 25, 1934. Shortly after her birth, Gloria and family moved to Scranton, Pennsylvania, the home of her childhood.

As a very young child, three years of age, Gloria was singing and performing for family and friends as well as community gatherings. By age 12, she was studying voice with well-known operatic coach Madame Lean Russell in New York. Madame Russell, after training Gloria for a while, heard that famed movie producer Joe Pasternak was in New York to audition young girls for a starring role in *The Under-Pup* for Universal Pictures. Mr. Pasternak had discovered one of Universal's biggest stars, Deanna Durbin.

Gloria won the audition, Pasternak loved her. So, in December 1938, Gloria and her mother arrived in Hollywood to start Gloria's movie career, which spanned the next 22 years. Soon after they arrived in Hollywood, Gloria's father and sisters joined them.

Gloria Jean made over 25 feature films at Universal Studios, co-starring with such stars as Donald O'Connor, W. C. Fields, Bing Crosby and Kirby Grant.

On the radio she appeared with Fred Allen, Edgar Bergen & Charlie McCarthy and a few of her movie co-stars, Bing Crosby, W. C. Fields, etc. She did several *Lux Radio Theater* programs and continued to make many, many personal appearances throughout the country.

Gloria in the early '60s had more or less retired from films and recordings. Together, Gloria and I decided to see what was available out there, which she would enjoy doing.

In the early eighties we became client and manager. The business had changed since her days at Universal, but I found casting directors and producers very interested in Gloria.

Gloria and I had lunch with well-known casting directors, met producers and generally tested the waters. By this time in Gloria's life, she had another career with Paula Kent, owner of Redkin Laboratories in the San Fernando Valley, also home of Universal Studios. Gloria had a wonderful and very interesting position with Redkin and soon became spokeswoman for the company.

As I said, Hollywood was changing; we were at the tail-end of the so-called Golden era. The studio system that Gloria grew up with was a passing scene. Because she was Gloria Jean, we could not find the scripts of interest that would make Gloria choose leaving her solid position at Redkin and, I, as her friend, would not want her to jeopardize her position. We soon dissolved our business relationship, but not our friendship which has endured and grows stronger with time. Gloria and her sister Bonnie, remain, to this day, two of my and Ellie's dearest and most valued friends. We share E-Mail, phone calls and news about our families.

I often wonder if the business hadn't changed, if Gloria Jean might not have remained one of Hollywood's constant stars. She still has her beauty and sweet personality. Gloria and Bonnie, Ellie and I love you.

See her credits as follows:

THE FILMS OF GLORIA JEAN

The Under-Pup 1939

If I Had My Way 1940

A Little Bit of Heaven 1940

Never Give a Sucker an Even Break 1941

What's Cookin'? 1942

Get Hep to Love 1942

When Johnny Comes Marching Home 1942

It Comes Up Love 1943

Mister Big 1943

Moonlight in Vermont 1943

Follow the Boys 1944

Pardon My Rhythm 1944

Ghost Catchers 1944

Reckless Age 1944

Destiny 1944

I'll Remember April 1945

River Gang 1945

Easy to Look At 1945

Copacabana 1947

I Surrender Dear 1948

An Old-Fashioned Girl 1949

THE FILMS OF GLORIA JEAN (Cont.)

Manhattan Angel 1949

There's a Girl in My Heart 1950

Air Strike 1955

Laffing Time 1959

The Ladies Man 1961

GLORIA JEAN'S DISCOGRAPHY

78 RPM RELEASES

Decca – 15047 – Lo! Hear the Gentle Lark 1939
Decca – 15047 – I'm Like a Bird 1939

Decca – 3116 – Penguin Song 1939
Decca – 3116 – Annie Laurie 1939

Decca – 3117 – Love's Old Sweet Song 1939
Decca – 3117 – Villanelle 1939

Decca – 3449 – A Little Big of Heaven 1940
Decca – 3449 – After Ev'ry Rainstorm 1940

CHAPTER 14

Bill Erwin
Ken Edwards

IN THE LATE 1970S, MY CLIENT STUART HAMBLEN HAD NARRATED A film, *Mountain Lady*, for producer Dan Quick and his company, Skyline Productions. Dan was now preparing the production of his script *Tough Men*, to be filmed in Alaska. I liked the script and wanted a young unknown actor I had just signed to play the young male lead. I told Dan about my client Ken Edwards. He had his reservations. As I explained, I had just signed Ken and he had no credits. I knew Ken would be up to the challenge, if he was given the chance.

It took a few meetings with Dan, but I finally sold him on the idea of hiring Ken for the male lead of "Corky." There was one big stipulation due to the fact that Ken was new in the business. They would want me to come to Alaska to help Ken and work with him on his acting. I would need to be on location with them for at least one week to 10 days. How could I manage? I had several deals in the works for my other clients. Through much planning, I arranged to be gone from my office for at least 10 days. I had never been to Alaska, so this was an awesome idea, a brand-new adventure.

Dan explained they had not cast the part of the older man, "Pappy." I knew the perfect actor for the role, but, wait, Bill Erwin and his wife Fran were friends but Bill was not represented by me.

Bill had worked in films, TV and radio for many, many years. A great character actor, you can see him in the Christopher Reeve picture *Somewhere in Time.*

Bill and I became acquainted through his wife Fran, who was the TV editor for the Daily News in the San Fernando Valley. Fran gave my clients good coverage and had Anacani on the cover (August 1979) of the TV Guide. I went to Bill, made my sales pitch on doing the film. Bill liked the idea. He, in turn, talked to his agent and his agent gave him the okay and his blessings to do the film for me and Dan.

Now Dan had his two main leads, Bill and Ken, and I had the journey from Los Angeles to Anchorage, Alaska. In September 1979, the three of us, Bill, Ken and myself, boarded a DC10 in Los Angeles, headed for the city of Anchorage, Alaska. We had a direct flight to Anchorage, about a 5-hour flight.

Upon our arrival in Anchorage, I was thinking we would have one mile in town and then in the morning we would fly to Port Elsworth, located on Lake Clark. This was not to be, as we were met at the airport on our arrival in Anchorage.

A bush pilot would fly us in a small plane to Lake Clark, where we would have our dinner and be put up there for the night. The plane only held four people, very cramped space at best. We took off from Anchorage Airport and the three of us were taking our first flight in a small aircraft. I think I held my breath all the way. I know I prayed.

We landed without incident at Lake Clark and motored to the bed and breakfast farmhouse that was our housing for the night. I'm not sure what we had for dinner, as by this time I was so tired and I'm sure Ken and Bill were too. Night came and I fell asleep very quickly. Morning seemed to come much too early. We had to be up bright and early (by 6:00 A.M. as I recall) to catch our flight by a float plane to the film location where Dan and the crew awaited us.

Again, a new experience. Neither I nor the other two had been on a float plane before. The float plane was necessary as we would land in water. Landing at Kontrashibuna, it looked like the mountain in the old Paramount Pictures logo, rising stately in the near distance. A body of water surrounded by tundra, trees and mountains and I was told no man had ever walked this virgin land.

Well, here we were, completely isolated from civilization except for the production crew. We were taken to the cook's tent and for the remaining days at Kontrashibuna, we would eat moose chili, moose burgers, moose stew, etc. It was my first time eating moose meat. I found it to be quite good. It must have been good; I gained several pounds in those few days. Upon my arrival back to Los Angeles, Ellie certainly noticed.

The weather was clear and beautiful, but cold; approximately 47 during the daylight hours, and as low as the 20s at night. We slept in tents. Bill, Ken and I were assigned our tent and I got claustrophobia one night, when as I woke up during the night the roof of our tent was down in my face.

The condensation had put weight on the tent. I had to get up out of my sleeping bag and walk out into the night to get fresh air. What a night, the stars were so bright and clear and the air so clean and crisp. From day one, we knew the flying gnats were a huge problem. We had to wear bug spray on our skin at all times. This was surely going to be one rough location shoot!

Day two was the first day of filming. Bill, Ken and the cutest, sweetest red and white Basset hound named Beauregard. From the initial day of filming, we knew that Bill had the role of "Pappy" under control. After all, Bill had years of experience and was a professional. To great surprise, Ken was up to the task at hand. His very first role on film and you would have thought he had several roles under his belt. He made "Corky" come to life. I knew he had the makings of a good actor.

I was so proud and relieved that I had made the decision to represent Ken. I had a find on my hands. Dan was very pleased with Ken's work.

The days at Kontrashibuna filming proved to be just what Dan wanted for this movie. We were finished at this location, time to fly back to Anchorage and then on to Soldotna. We were flown back via an Aero Commander plane. Looking from either side of the plant, I had never seen so much snow and ice-capped mountains, just as far as the eyes could see.

The pilot quizzed us on our days on location and seemed thoroughly interested in the film. He questioned, "So you had no radio or any outside communication while you were on location? Then you guys probably haven't heard about the terrible plane crash near San Diego?"

He told us about the awful crash that had happened while we were on location. The crash happened in or near San Diego, California. Here we are, told about this while in the plane, with nothing below us but mountains, mountains and more mountains, icy and snow capped. If we were to crash, no one would find us for days. God saw that we landed in Anchorage and was I glad to feel ground under my feet. I know Ken and Bill must have felt the same way.

We had dinner in Anchorage and then flew to Soldotna. We had a day off, so Dan showed us around Soldotna. Everywhere you looked, the stores, churches and landmarks that we could see, you could feel the Russian-influence in architect.

The guys were to go to a new location to finish the film and I would travel to Kenai to fly to Anchorage and then from Anchorage back to Seattle, Washington to catch a flight from Seattle and arrive back at LAX at about 1:00 A.M. I was needed back at my office to handle business for my other clients. I must say, Los Angeles looked awfully good to me. But, what an adventure I had just been on!

I can't think of too many careers that would have afforded me travel, adventure, meeting new and wonderful people and what an education in itself. The film was finished and now Bill and Ken came home to Los Angeles.

While writing about this part of my career, my family and I recently viewed *Tough Men*. A very fine film and I was moved deeply recalling those times. Bill and I remain good friends. I'm not sure of Ken's whereabouts. He was a wonderful young man.

CHAPTER 15

KATHRYN GRAYSON

Voice of an Angel

Grace of a special Lady

A Dear Friend

IN THE MID-1980S, A MUTUAL FRIEND OF DALE EVANS' AND MINE CALLED my office and explained that she was in fact a good friend of actress/singer Kathryn Grayson and Kathryn would like me to come to her home to discuss my management. I had never met Kathryn, but like so many people, I had seen her in films and one of my personal favorites was MGM's *Rio Rita*, with Bud Abbott, Lou Costello and John Carroll.

I always did my homework on potential clients, and Kathryn would be no different. I learned Kathryn was born in Winston-Salem, North Carolina, on February 02, 1922. She was signed to an MGM Studios contract in early 1941. She made her film debut in *Andy Hardy's Private Secretary* in 1941.

During her time at MGM, she starred in many of their most popular films: *Seven Sweethearts, Two Sisters from Boston, It Happened in Brooklyn* (another favorite of mine), *Show Boat, So This is Love, That Midnight Kiss, The Toast of New Orleans,* and *Kiss Me Kate.* She also starred in Warner Brothers' *The Desert Song* and *The Vagabond King* for Paramount.

During these years, Kathryn married twice. Her first husband was actor John Shelton in 1940. They divorced in 1946. In 1947, she married actor/singer Johnnie Johnston. They had one child, a daughter, Patricia, in 1951. The Johnstons were divorced.

I made a call to Kathryn and she invited Ellie and me to her home the following Saturday afternoon, the same home she has been living in for 61 years as of 2006. We lived in Sherman Oaks, California at the time and the drive to Kathryn's home in Santa Monica would take about 30 to 40 minutes. As we drove over the canyon from the San Fernando Valley to Santa Monica, I was thinking, Kathryn is a legend, a huge star of the '40s and '50s, would we click?

Upon our arrival to her beautiful estate, we were greeted at the door by Sally Sherman, Kathryn's longtime secretary and dear friend. Sally was very warm and spoke in a definite Australian accent. We learned she was in fact Australian. We were asked to please be seated in the foyer and Miss Grayson would soon join us. Soon, the beautiful, very charming Kathryn Grayson joined us. I liked her instantly. Ellie told me later that she had felt the same way.

It helped a lot that Kathryn liked Dale very much and we soon realized we had a few mutual friends and acquaintances. That very first meeting we had a wonderful conversation and got to know each other. It would be a pleasure to represent Kathryn, so, we agreed to give it a try.

Many visits followed our initial meeting and we became good friends. I believe our second visit to her home, Kathryn, Sally, Ellie and I went to lunch. Kathryn treated.

During the time that Kathryn and I worked together, I had her on *Entertainment Tonight* interviewed by Mary Hart (very beautiful lady) and John Tesh, who went on to be quite a musician and recording artist.

I saw a script on the Angela Lansbury series *Murder, She Wrote* on CBS-TV, and contacted the casting director, Ron Stephenson, and made my pitch on Kathryn's behalf. Ron wanted Kathryn for the part and, in 1987, Kathryn guest starred on episode #72, "If It's Thursday, It Must Be Beverly," as "Ideal Malloy." She was to do two more episodes as "Ideal Malloy," "The Sins of Castle Cove" and "Town Father" through December 1989. I felt we were getting off to a good start, but Kathryn decided she wanted some time out to start a book about her fabulous career.

Kathryn and I were friends, this was fine with me. Kathryn has done several live shows from time to time since we parted company. In the 1990s she appeared with her MGM friend Van Johnson in the play *Love Letters*. She also has done her one woman show, *An Evening with Kathryn Grayson*.

Kathryn, Sally, Ellie and I remain friends and I cherish my time working with Miss Grayson.

CHAPTER 16

It Has Been a Long and Happy Journey

IN THE LATE 1990S I BEGAN TO SLOW DOWN AND WAS THINKING ABOUT my retirement in early 2000. It had been a long and successful run, using a show business expression.

Ellie and I moved away from the Hollywood scene and retired to a small community about 35 miles from Hollywood. One of my new neighbors was Cliffie Stone (former manager of Tennessee Ernie Ford, Molly Bee, etc.) I had known Cliffie for years. He as a youngster, had been a member of Stuart Hamblen's band and in later years had become a manager and record producer. (He produced one of Dale's recordings.)

Cliffie and I would have breakfast out at some local restaurant about two to three times weekly. We enjoyed revisiting our careers. Cliffie commented one morning at breakfast that he and I should start a new management company and call it the 100-Year Management Company. Thinking of my years and his years as managers combined. A little stretch, but we had a big laugh out of this.

Cliffie passed away suddenly on January 17, 1998. My dear friend was gone, but not forgotten. I miss him and our friendship.

This was the year Ellie and I had many losses. Her beloved mother Edna Landis, my oldest sister Jean, our dear friend Roy Rogers and a good neighbor, actor, trick roper, Montie Montana all passed away. And, while writing my memoirs, on November 8, 2006, Ellie's dear and beloved sister, Edna Jeanne died suddenly. Our love for each other and our faith has sustained us.

After my retirement, I continued to advise and counsel a few artists, mostly my close friends.

AND ALONG THE WAY

Back in the early sixties, I was at my bank, Security Pacific Bank in Studio City, California, in line to do some banking business. The gentleman just ahead of me was none other than Bob Nolan, one of the founders, along with Roy Rogers, of the Sons of the Pioneers. He turned around and said something to me (I don't recall what). Even though I was friends with Roy & Dale and also Stuart Hamblen (Bob and Stuart were longtime friends), this was the first and only time I had ever met Bob Nolan. He seemed like a very kind and gentle man. I was very impressed.

IN CONCLUSION

WRITING THE MEMOIRS OF MY CAREER IN HOLLYWOOD, I WONDER how I did so much and how fascinating and extraordinary by life has really been. Dale Evans, Stuart Hamblen, Roy Rogers, Jr., Anacani, Frontiersman & Joanie and all the other wonderfully talented people who have touched my life, have made the journey fun and exciting.

I thank the dear Lord for giving me these opportunities and giving me courage, faith and not to be afraid to work hard and always try to be fair and honest. I thank Him for giving me Ellie in my life and a wonderful supportive family and all those dear friends along the way. Friends like Kerry Ross, an actor/magician who still consults with me. Kerry and I have been friends since the mid-1970s. We met at our mutual photographer Bob Bucher's studios in North Hollywood.

Bill & Doneen Nolt (Bill is a Roy Rogers lookalike and attends many Western film festivals), actress Myrna Dell, who I've known since 1962, and so many other wonderful people.

DICK BAXTER

BIBLIOGRAPHY

Western Horseman Magazine: May 1965, model for Viola Grae Western Wear (ad & photo)

Various trade publications: (*The Hollywood Reporter, Variety,* etc., 1966 through 1980s)

Fan magazines, various (1970 thru 1980s)

Daily News: Several times thru the '70s and '80s – articles & photos

Mexican publications: various, with client Anacani – articles & photos

Amusement Business: Feature, *Dick Baxter Says,* 1980s

Studio Magazine, 1969

San Fernando Valley Que Magazine, 1967

Oak Tree Express Magazine: 2 articles, 1980s

Roy Rogers & Dale Evans: Tribute to Dale Evans written by Dick Baxter

Cowboys & Indians, Fall 2001: Picture with client Dale Evans, pg. 30

Classic Images, 2001: Tribute to Dale Evans by Dick Baxter

Mountain Signal, Sept 2003: Feature story by Flo Price with many photos, b&w & color

Classic Images: Full-page feature, *Letter to Dale by Dick Baxter*, photo, Dick & Dale

Tehachapi News, 2000: Feature by Bill Mead

Tehachapi News: Feature, lots of Photos by Joy Mazola

National Newspaper: Bonnie Churchill, Marilyn Beck & various others

Kingsbury's Who's Who in Country Music (book): Bio & photo, 1970s

Sing Your Heart Out, Country Boy: Mentioned with client Stuart Hamblen, 1970s

Platinum Rainbow (book), December 1980

Shaking Hands with Fame by Osie Jackson & Linda L. Woody: Mentioned & photos, 2006

Roy Rogers "King of the Cowboys" & Dale Evans, "Queen of the West": Comment by Dick Baxter on back cover, September 2006

Mountain Signal (newspaper), "A Dream That Came True," article with photo of Dick and Ellie Baxter, April 2000

RADIO & TV

Baxter's Bag: Guests Marty Allen & Joanie Summers – 1960s

Dick Baxter Show: Guest singer Patti Spangler

Chronicle of the Old West: Interview, Show #132, June 2007

QUOTES AND TIDBITS

ROY ROGERS said, "Don't ever tell Dale and me something you don't want remembered." He claimed, "We have memories like an elephant."

ROY "DUSTY" ROGERS gave me a pin badge one year for my birthday; it read, "Best Manager." Also, he and Linda gave me a silver keychain shaped like a spur (quite heavy). I cherish both gifts to this day.

STUART HAMBLEN – When I would call Stuart by phone, I would always ask, "Stuart, how are you doing?" He would always reply, "Cooking on the front burner." I miss those calls.

BILL ERWIN – When I phone Bill, he always says, "Oh, my friend that took me to Alaska to freeze to death." (A reference to the movie *Tough Men*.)

GLORIA JEAN – Speaking of my long career says, "It's like a stripe on your sleeve that you will wear the rest of your life."

SUZY HAMBLEN said I was one of the best idea persons she ever knew. Thank you, Suzy.

ROY ROGERS – Though we were friends for over 40 years, he always called me by my birth name, Richard. Dale and Dusty never did.

DALE EVANS – Dale to me at airports and busy places: "Keep moving, they can't hit a moving target."

DALE EVANS – She always said that she and I were "a couple of pauses."

BILL ERWIN – Always liked to see me in my dark-green sport coat. He said it represented success and money.

ANACANI – Tried to teach me Spanish. I'm afraid that my Spanish remains pretty bad. Poor Anacani, she tried.

DALE EVANS – California Mother of the Year, 1967

DALE EVANS – Texas Woman of the Year, 1970

DALE EVANS – Inducted into the Cowgirl Hall of Fame, 1995

DALE EVANS – Recipient of Cardinal Terrance Cook's Humanities Award, 1995

DALE EVANS – Has two stars on the Hollywood Walk of Fame, Hollywood, California

ROY ROGERS – Leaving a restaurant in Sherman Oaks, California one evening, Roy put his hand on my shoulder and said, "Richard, if at the end of the day you have one true friend you can count on, you are truly blessed." Wisdom from the King of the Cowboys.

SAM LOVULLO – producer of the Hee Haw TV show: "Dale Evans had the creative juices to orchestrate the best performances for herself and Roy. She knew what the audience wanted to hear and see."

DALE EVANS – Response to me regarding her one-woman show, "I'm like a female Victor Borge, except I try not to fall off the piano bench."

WILL HUTCHINS – TV's Sugarfoot: "Dick Baxter is a true son of the West, straight shooter, a dying breed out thar in LaLa Land. Dick, Ellie, Babs [Will's wife] and I share a love of the heyday of Hollywood."

"DON'T EVER FORGET ME AND ALWAYS REMEMBER YOU ARE MY BABY BROTHER."

Dale's last words to me, shortly before her passing.

DICK BAXTER

ABOUT THE AUTHOR

Dick Baxter is a retired Personal Manager (1963-2003), who managed some of Hollywood's brightest stars: Dale Evans, Stuart Hamblen, Anacani, and others.

He is still active with his music publishing company, Dick Baxter Publishing Company (ASCAP). Among the songs he has written are "The Miracle of Miracles" and "Promises to Keep." Dick has been married to his wife Ellie for 51 years. They were married in 1955.

Ellie was employed 17 years at NBC-TV in Burbank, California.

The Baxters live in Southern California and share their mini-ranch with their Corgi dog named "Rodney."

Printed in the United States
88164LV00005B/6/A